HOME NETWORKING
SOLUTIONS

Paul Heltzel

Praise for Paul Heltzel's
Home Networking Solutions

"*Home Networking Solutions* is one of the best networking books I have read; it is easy to follow and easy to use. I will always keep a copy of this book in my home library for reference."
Donna Meyer, home networking novice

"*Home Networking Solutions* is a great book for everyone who wants to build a home network but isn't quite sure where to start. Intelligently written, it caters to people with all levels of computer skills, taking them through selecting the equipment, building the network, and troubleshooting those problems that always arise when plugging everything together."

"Covering all common home networking setups—whether you want to get a few PCs together for games or surf the web from your sofa using the latest in wireless technology—*Home Networking Solutions* has the answer to your questions."

"Having shown the book to a colleague who has been trying to set up a network at home, it was obvious how well the concepts are explained. After several weeks of frustration, he read the book and, by the end of a weekend, had transformed his collection of three PCs into a network to share his printer and Internet connection. On top of this, he is now confident that it's secure from the outside world and that he can keep it that way because he understands how everything works."
Richard Busby, network technician

"An excellent introduction and overview of current networking technologies for the home user. With a little patience, familiarity with basic computing principles, and the resources cited in this book, nearly anyone should be able to set up, configure, and maintain their own home networking solution. An easy and informative read."
Jim Killian, independent software developer

"This book is a definitive reference work and text in the home networking field. Paul Heltzel has captured the essence of home networking from wired to wireless. Divided into thirteen easy-to-follow chapters, the book begins with networking basics and winds up with discussions about security and operating system specifics. An added plus are discussions on the utilization of home networks. These discussions will entice more home PC users to explore the capabilities of home networking."
Howard Vaux, systems builder and large systems project manager

"Mr. Heltzel tackles that most promising and intimidating of projects—networking your computers at home—and provides a plain English, step-by-step guide that is truly indispensable. It's an amazing example of how even the most tangled process can be cleaned up by a skilled writer. We need to get Mr. Heltzel to take on the U.S. Tax Code next."
Glenn McDonald, a freelance technology writer who has written for PC World, CNET, MIT Technology Review, Family PC, and CNN

"As more and more people set up home offices, Heltzel's lucid and accessible guide will be indispensable."
David Cameron, staff editor, MIT's Technology Review magazine

"A great up-to-date and informative tool for those just starting out and those already in networking."
Phil Barbier, web developer & network administrative engineer

"Very informative. Definitely, a must-read for anyone contemplating setting up a network in the home or small office! Especially useful for beginners."
Adolfo Reyes, home networking enthusiast

"*Home Networking Solutions* is terrific! This book is fast, concise, and non-technical. I recommend it to anyone who wants to learn networking quickly."
Jean Doyon, IT student

Home Networking Solutions

Credits: Senior Editor, Mark Garvey; Production Editor, Rodney A. Wilson; Copyeditor, Karen Annett; Graphics Coordinator, Deborah Bone; Cover Design, Chad Planner, *Pop Design Works*; Interior Design and Layout, *GEX Publishing Services*; Indexer, Kevin Broccoli, *Broccoli Information Management*.

Publisher: Andy Shafran

Library of Congress Catalog Number: 2002105478

ISBN 1-929685-51-3

1   2   3   4   5   WC   05   04   03   02

MUSKA & LIPMAN

Muska & Lipman Publishing

2645 Erie Avenue, Suite 41

Cincinnati, Ohio 45208

www.muskalipman.com

publisher@muskalipman.com

About the Author

Paul Heltzel, a seasoned technology journalist, has contributed an impressive list of computer-related articles for such magazines and Web sites as *CNN Interactive*, *PC World Magazine*, and *MIT Technology Review*. Moreover, he has written for the tech sections of *The Washington Post* and *The New York Times on the Web*. When not busy networking computers at home, Paul writes and travels with his wife, dog, and his mobile office, a 1969 Safari Airstream camper with its own wireless network. *Home Networking Solutions* is his fourth book.

Acknowledgments

Working with the crew at Muska & Lipman has been great. Thanks to Andy Shafran for the opportunity to write this book. Thanks especially to Mark Garvey for smart edits, and to Sherri Schwartz, Kris White, and Rodney Wilson for making sure the book gets into people's hands. Thanks to Karen Annett for her sharp attention to detail, and to Jim Killian, Richard Busby, and P.J. Grinsel for scrupulous fact checking. Neil Salkind, my agent at Studio B, gets another tip of the hat for finding me more good work. Finally, I can't say thanks enough to my wife Deborah, who expertly handles a million jobs, from working with me on the table of contents (in Denver) to obtaining artwork (in D.C.) and editing my text (in New Orleans). Thanks for keeping things moving, Deb.

Dedication

For my mom, Gretchen, and for Nachin, who told me to write something complimentary. You guys rock!

Introduction

Home networking used to be a hobby for geeks (like me) who didn't mind taking a weekend to get the job done. No longer. With new technologies that make home networking simple, you can set aside an afternoon and start sharing Internet access, files, printers, games, and MP3s. Networking computers at home really is straightforward, especially when you approach the task in simple steps, without using lots of jargon.

So, why should you network your home? It's a fair question, as you've probably been doing just fine up until now. Fine, that is, except that your phone is busy when someone uses the Internet, and you can't access a printer upstairs from your computer downstairs, and you use floppies to transfer files. These are the symptoms of a home that needs a network—now.

This book can help. Whether you want to use wireless technology that lets you take your laptop around (or outside), or use an electrical outlet or phone jack to connect your computers together, *Home Networking Solutions* offers guidance and tips.

What You Can Do

A home network can be used for sharing all sorts of data, and for getting more use and more fun out of your computers.

▶ You can share Internet access on all your computers. Whether you use the modem that came with your PC or a fast broadband (cable or DSL) connection, everyone in your house can surf at the same time.

▶ In addition to sharing Internet access, you can share files and printers, using wireless, or "no-new-wires" networking hardware that shares data over the existing wiring in your house. No stringing cables for you.

▶ You can play games, and music, on any computer in your house. The kids can battle each other in networked multiplayer games, and you can listen to your favorite MP3 audio files over your network, like a computerized jukebox anywhere you have a PC.

Who This Book is For

This book is for anyone who wants to start getting more use out of their computers. However, if you fit any of the following descriptions, this book will be ideal for you.

▶ You want to network your computers and want step-by-step directions, rather than long-winded explanations of technology you might never use.

▶ You want more flexibility in choosing where you want to use your computers.

▶ You think some of the speed and convenience of your office network would be useful at home (or in your home office).

How This Book Works

This book, like the others in the Muska & Lipman Solutions series, is focused on getting the job done. We don't concentrate on the networking equipment of a particular vendor, though in some cases, in keeping with a step-by-step approach, we have used specific equipment and software as a case study. In these cases, an attempt has been made to be precise in the steps but general in guidance, so that you will find the tips and advice in this book helpful no matter what networking equipment you purchase.

How This Book is Organized

Chapter 1, "Network Overview." What is a network and how can you use it? Here we look at how networks work and how you can benefit from them. You also find out about setting up networks for different environments and what you can accomplish with a network.

Chapter 2, "Laying Out a Network." In this chapter you learn what equipment you need and where to put it. We also figure out what bandwidth means and how to expand your network with a device called a hub.

Chapter 3, "Installing Hardware." In this chapter, we step through physically installing different types of networks, including wireless, Ethernet, and phone and powerline networks. We also consider software that lets you share PCs and Macs.

Chapter 4, "Direct Connections." Find out how to connect two PCs using a cable when you need to move files or upgrade your computer.

Chapter 5, "Sharing Data and Equipment." In this chapter we'll walk through setting up your software to provide access to files and equipment. You can share printers, CD-ROM drives, hard drives, and other devices.

Chapter 6, "Sharing Video and Music." This chapter shows you how to enjoy music and watch Internet video on your network, from any computer in the house.

Chapter 7, "Do You Want to Play a Game?" Learn all about connecting over your network, and over the Internet, to play multiplayer games. You can join computers online or host a game on your own PC.

Chapter 8, "Sharing the Internet." This chapter walks you through setting up your home network to share access to the Internet.

Chapter 9, "Remote Access." What good is a network when you're on the road? Here you learn how to access files at home from the office or office files from home. Using these tips you can create a fast and rewarding telecommuting setup.

Chapter 10, "Security." Taking care of business at home. In this chapter we look at security measures that can help keep your network safe.

Chapter 11, "Troubleshooting." Here we consider common problems and how to fix them. You'll learn how to bypass everyday hang-ups and back up your network to avoid data disaster.

Chapter 12, "Upgrading." In this chapter you'll learn about ways to expand and upgrade your network. We'll also consider whether you could use a server. If a server will help, you'll see how to simply set up a computer to share files.

Chapter 13, "Windows XP Case Study." In this networking how-to, we take you step by step through setting up Microsoft's latest operating system for sharing files, printers, and Internet access with Windows 95/98/2000/Me computers.

Appendix A, "Growing Your Network, a Visual Guide." Here you'll find a visual presentation of various ways to set up your network. These illustrations will show you how you can build up your network, adding equipment as you need it, over time. For each setup, you'll see how the hardware is connected, what components you'll need, and some of the benefits and drawbacks of each configuration.

Appendix B, "Glossary." A catch-all of terms and concepts related to home networking.

Appendix C, "Network Yellow Pages." When your kitchen sink sprouts a leak, you might open the Yellow Pages to find a plumber. Likewise, when you need networking help, or buying advice, you can turn to the sites listed here for assistance.

1

Network Overview

What is a network and how can you use one? In this chapter, we answer both of those questions and look at the basics of how to connect your computers at home. After reading Chapter 1, you should understand how networks work and what you need to do to get your computers communicating with each other. In later chapters, we go into more detail, providing hands-on advice and, of course, solutions.

First, we look at how computers communicate with each other over home networks. Then, we check out the benefits and drawbacks of each type of networking technology (wireless vs. wired, for instance) so you can get a feel for what will work best for you.

In an ideal world, you just plug in all your networking hardware and get to work. In rare cases—similar to making a hole in one—it really is just that simple. To make sure things go smoothly, we make sure you know how to take the simplest path to creating your home network, avoiding common pitfalls that can make the job seem daunting. First, though, we provide a simple explanation of how a network works.

Understanding How Networks Work

If you're not currently using a network at home, it's hard to imagine how a network will speed up and simplify your day-to-day work with computers.

Consider how much more effective—and fun—your computer is once you connect to the Internet. Because the Internet is simply a very large network that connects many networks, you already have a sense of how much more you can do with a network than with a solitary PC. Connecting your computers makes your computers work together like a smoothly flowing thoroughfare.

What Is a Network?

For our purposes, a home network is two or more computers that are connected by cables or wireless radio transmitters, allowing the computers to transmit information to each other. You can use a network to transmit and share all sorts of data, including Internet access and files on your computer, such as video and audio files; you can access files from one computer and watch and listen on another.

Here, we look at some basic terms that often come up when discussing networks. You'll get a further understanding of them as we discuss them in context. In the meantime, these are a handful of the most important networking terms. You'll get enough of a feel for them here that you could use them in a cocktail party conversation with the network guy at work. Of course, if you work at home, that might be you. Onward.

▶ **Network adapter**. To get your network started, you obviously need to physically connect your computers together. First, you need a network adapter for each computer. A network adapter is a device you plug into your PC that enables communication between computers. Network adapters are sometimes called NICs, or Network Interface Cards.

▶ **Ethernet**. Most office networks use Ethernet. Ethernet is a standard, sometimes called an architecture, for network communication and, more casually, what most people call networks that use Ethernet hardware. The cabling for an Ethernet network looks a lot like telephone cable; however, it is thicker and has eight wires inside the cable instead of four. The cheapest and most often used Ethernet network hardware is called 10BaseT, which transmits data at up to 10 mbps (megabits per second). Newer—and more expensive—Ethernet hardware, called 100BaseT, transmits data at 100 mbps.

▶ **Hub**. You can use a hub to connect multiple computers to one network. A hub looks like a box with open ports on it (the open ports look similar to telephone jacks). You run a cable from the hub to your computer. At your computer, you plug the cable into your network adapter.

If you only had these elements, a PC running Windows 95 or later, and some free time, you could start a network. If you're really in a rush, read this chapter, then jump to Chapter 5, "Sharing Data and Equipment." Chapter 5 tells you how to set up Windows to share files and printers. After following the advice in these two chapters, you'll have a network— hopefully, a running network! If not, you should check out Chapter 11, "Troubleshooting," to figure out what's wrong.

In between these chapters, you find out how to do more complicated tasks, such as sharing Internet access (Chapter 8, "Sharing the Internet"), and simpler ones, too, such as connecting two computers directly to exchange a few files (Chapter 4, "Direct Connections").

If you plan to set up a wireless network or want to share Internet access, you need more equipment.

CHAPTER 1

▶ **Router**. If you plan to share Internet access, you'll probably want a router. Routers let one network communicate with another. In most cases in home networking, this means connecting the computer network at your house to the very large network called the Internet. You can also use a built-in feature of Windows, called Internet Connection Sharing, to share Internet access between your computers. This setup, however, requires a computer dedicated to the task. So, in general, we recommend using a router. Your Internet Service Provider (ISP) might also be able to provide you with Internet access for multiple computers; however, this service usually comes at a higher monthly cost than standard service. Typically, using a router, you can connect as many computers as you want to one Internet account.

▶ **Wireless access point**. If you decide to start a wireless network, you should consider an access point. An access point works a bit like a wireless hub, allowing multiple computers with wireless network adapters to communicate with each other. An access point also lets you connect a wireless network to a wired one, or to a cable or DSL (Digital Subscriber Line) modem. If you purchase a wireless access point, it's a good idea to buy one with a built-in router.

VARIOUS TYPES OF NETWORKS

Most home networks are considered peer-to-peer networks, meaning they connect to each other directly. Many office networks use a central computer, called a server, for storing files or programs that everyone can share. A server-based network is often called a client-server network. This book concentrates on simple peer-to-peer networks. In the final chapter of this book, Chapter 12 ("Upgrading"), you find out how a server might help your network, but most of the day-to-day functions of home networking, such as sharing files, printers, and Internet access, won't require you to set up a server.

How Do Computers Communicate over a Network?

On the hardware side, network adapters, or Network Interface Cards (NICs), control the flow of data through cables or, if you set up a wireless network, through radio signals. Personal computers come with the software necessary to network. So, you don't need to invest a fortune in software to get your computers talking with each other and sharing files.

Network communication is enabled on the software side by installing a networking language with a few clicks. The language you use is called a *protocol*. Your network adapter might configure the protocol for you, or you might need to configure the protocol yourself. (For more information, see Chapter 5, "Sharing Data and Equipment.") You don't need to know how protocols work to use them, just as you don't need to know how electricity works to plug in a lamp. But, it's not a bad idea to know up-front that protocols enable communication over a network.

A protocol establishes rules about how computers communicate. You may have heard the acronym TCP (Transmission Control Protocol), which is the lingua franca of the Internet and makes a fine protocol for file and printer sharing, as well as sharing Internet access, over your home network.

Here's an example of how computers trade information over a network using a protocol.

▶ Computer 1: I want to send some data.

▶ Computer 2: Ready.

▶ Computer 1: Did you get the data?

▶ Computer 2: I've received the data.

If you have more than two computers, you can plug a cable from your computer's network adapter to a *hub*, a hardware device with ports (see Figure 1.1). A hub lets you connect as many computers to your network as the hub has available ports (usually four to sixteen). We talk more about hubs in Chapter 2, "Laying Out a Network," and Chapter 3, "Installing Hardware."

Figure 1.1
A hub lets you connect multiple computers to your network

LOCAL AREA NETWORKS

A network within one home or office is often called a LAN (Local Area Network). LANs are used to share data and peripherals, such as printers, CD-ROM drives, and tape backup drives, as well as Internet access.

Getting Started: Types of Networks

Getting a network up and running can be as simple as setting aside half an hour to connect a cable between two computers and then selecting a few options to change the network settings on your PC.

Or, if you have a free afternoon, you can connect all the computers in your house and share an Internet connection. If you have DSL or cable Internet access, you can connect to the Net and keep your phone line free.

First, you should figure out what networking technology you want to use.

The biggest decision to make is what kind of network to install—wired or wireless. If you decide to go wired, you can use Ethernet network hardware from a variety of manufacturers, including Intel, 3Com, Netgear, and Linksys. For those of you who decide to use a wireless network, you can choose from many vendors, such as Netgear, Linksys, D-Link, or Proxim.

Other choices exist for starting a network without installing new wires in your home. Some network equipment makers now sell special equipment that allows you to connect through your home's phone or electrical wiring. Phoneline and powerline networks can save you lots of time and trouble, but they are not as widely used as Ethernet.

The most common types of home networking products include:

> ▶ **Ethernet**. The most widely used, and some say most reliable, network type is Ethernet. It's fast (10 to 100 mbps per second), inexpensive, and uses connectors called RJ-45 that look like, but are slightly larger than, regular telephone connectors. Most office networks are connected using Ethernet. Up until a few years ago, Ethernet was pretty much the only game in town if you wanted to wire your PCs together.

> ▶ **Wireless**. Networks using wireless technology have really taken off. It's no wonder, because wireless networking is plenty fast for most home users. Initially, wireless equipment was very expensive, but it's becoming competitive in price with wired network technologies. Most importantly, wireless networks let you communicate through walls, doors, and glass without running cables. However, wireless networks are limited in how far they can transmit a signal. It's usually about 150 feet (sometimes less because the range is lessened by obstructions, such as walls, brick, and steel). Wireless network adapters can communicate directly with each other or through an access point, which acts like a wireless hub. For fast Internet access shared throughout the house, you can also connect your wireless network to a cable or DSL (Digital Subscriber Line) modem using an access point (see Figure 1.2).

CHAPTER 1

Figure 1.2
You can connect your wireless network to a cable or DSL modem using a wireless access point like this one from D-Link

▶ **Phoneline**. Often called HomePNA, phoneline networking lets you use your existing house telephone wiring to connect your network. You can purchase HomePNA products from vendors including Netgear, Linksys, and 3Com. Phoneline products are more expensive than Ethernet, but typically less expensive than wireless. You can connect regular phone wiring to a NIC that then connects to an available USB (Universal Serial Bus) port (Figure 1.3) on your desktop or laptop computer. You can also install the network card into an open PCI slot inside your desktop computer (Figure 1.4) or a PC Card slot on your laptop (Figure 1.5).

Figure 1.3
You can network computers using regular phone line and a network adapter, such as this phoneline USB version from Netgear

Figure 1.4
A phoneline PCI
networking adapter
needs to be installed by
opening the case of
your computer and
finding an available
PCI slot

Figure 1.5
PC Card phoneline
adapters let you add a
notebook to your
network (Photo
courtesy of the Linksys
Group, Inc. 2002)

▶ **Powerline**. Networking products that send data over the electrical wiring in
your house are relatively new. Previously, only one company produced a
powerline networking product, and it was quite slow. Faster powerline
networking products have recently become available, and they are very
promising because homes typically have more electrical outlets than phone
jacks. The number of electrical outlets in the average home makes setting up
computers in this way nearly as convenient as using wireless equipment.

▶ **Crossover cable.** A crossover cable is a special Ethernet cable you can purchase (from manufacturers including Belkin) to transfer files from one computer to another. This is especially helpful if you don't want to set up a whole network, but just need to trade an occasional file from one computer to another. Figure 1.6 shows a crossover cable.

Figure 1.6
A crossover cable lets you connect two PCs, which is useful when you don't want to set up an entire network but want to transfer files from one computer to another

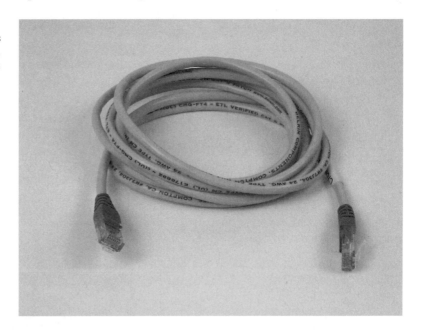

WIDE AREA NETWORKS

A large network that connects many, often geographically distant, networks is called a WAN (Wide Area Network). WANs are typically connected by fast phone lines, such as a T-1 (1.5 mbps) or T-3 (45 mbps). Don't confuse LANs, such as a home network, with WANs, even though they are often mentioned together. You don't need to know anything about WANs to set up a home network.

Where to Plug In: Types of Network Adapters

So, how do you get the network interface card connected to your PC? Depending on the type of computer you want to connect (desktop or laptop), you have several options when purchasing a network adapter.

Some network adapters are easier to install than others. The tradeoff for convenience might be speed, but in most home networking environments, the speed difference is inconsequential. In other words, you pretty much can't go wrong.

Whether you decide to go wired or wireless, you can connect your network adapter using USB, PCI (Peripheral Component Interconnect), and PC Card (sometimes called PCMCIA) interfaces. All the major manufacturers make products using each connection type.

USB

A USB connector allows you to plug into ports you probably already have in your computer, if you bought your PC later than 1995. USB makes sense for people who aren't comfortable opening a desktop computer case to install a network interface card. USB networking products can transfer data at a maximum of 12 mbps. Figure 1.7 shows a USB network adapter for an Ethernet network. The device allows you to plug an Ethernet cable into a USB port on your computer.

Figure 1.7
A USB adapter from Linksys allows you to plug an Ethernet cable into an available USB port on your computer (Photo courtesy of the Linksys Group, Inc. 2002)

PCI

Installing a PCI card offers greater speed but less convenience. You need to open your computer case and find an open PCI slot to install the network card. It's not hard science, but it takes more time than installing a USB card. People who are comfortable installing hardware in their computers might favor a PCI network adapter because once you install it, there's no chance of accidentally pulling it out and disconnecting your connection. In addition, the USB ports on some computers (there are usually two) are found on the front of the computer. Some might appreciate keeping their network cabling out of sight. PCI Ethernet adapters offer the best speed of any product mentioned here: 100 mbps. Figure 1.8 shows a PCI network adapter card for a wireless network.

Figure 1.8
This wireless network adapter from Netgear connects to an internal PCI slot in a PC; after installing the PCI card in the computer, you must then insert a PC Card network adapter into the PC Card adapter—it's a bit more trouble than simply inserting a USB wireless networking adapter into an open USB port on your computer

PC Card

You can connect your laptop to a network using a PC Card. The small device slides into the PC Card slot on the side of a laptop. Installing a PC Card is as simple as installing a USB card, and a PC Card takes up less space. PC Card connections are also speedy: up to 132 mbps maximum data throughput. Figure 1.9 shows a PC Card wireless network adapter from D-Link. Pop the card into your PC Card slot and you're ready to go.

Figure 1.9
D-Link's wireless adapter card for a notebook computer slides into an open PC Card slot

MEASUREMENTS OF SPEED

Most network speed is measured in megabits per second (mbps). Internet connections are typically measured in kilobits per second (kbps) or, if they're very fast, such as a digital T-1 line in an office, megabits per second.

Who Needs a Network?

Networks can help just about anybody who uses a computer. If you have multiple PCs in the house that need to use the Internet, or if you want to share files in a small home office, the simplest of networks dramatically improves your work habits. If you're constantly hogging the Internet connection in your home, the life you save might be your own.

Some of the people who will especially benefit from setting up a network include:

▶ Gamers who want to connect to, and conquer, others by network, no matter where they are. Figures 1.10 and 1.11 show the networked versions of the computer games Civilization III and Quake III Arena. Network games are great when played over the network in your house, and very fun (though kind of odd) when played with strangers over the Internet.

▶ Multiple students in the house who need access to the Internet at the same time.

▶ Telecommuters who want to network a broadband modem and have fast Internet access at each computer, just like they have at work.

▶ Folks who are ready to jump into wireless networking so they can use a laptop to browse the Internet on a couch by the fireplace, or send e-mail or print a document from any room where they are most comfortable.

▶ Small office workers who carry files by hand (on floppy or CD) from one computer to another. If you're burning CDs to transfer files, you really, really need to spend an afternoon setting up a small network.

▶ A family with many PCs, but just one printer. You can purchase one good printer instead of three so-so ones. Everyone on the network can send documents to a printer attached to any other PC on the network.

SHARING SOFTWARE & FILES

Not all software can run over a network. The software must be designed to use over a network. Many companies use an office network to share software, such as Lotus Notes. Most folks using a home network don't need to share programs. You can install the program you want to use on each computer in the network. Then, if you want to share files created by the program, you can easily access the files over your network. Accessing files from a computer on your network is as simple as opening a file from the hard drive of the computer on which you're working.

Figure 1.10
Multiplayer computer
games, such as
Civilization III,
allow players to go
one-on-one

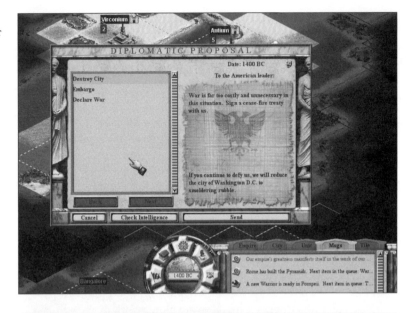

Figure 1.11
Quake III Arena allows
the more bloodthirsty
networkers to fight it
out online

Network Setups for Different Environments

The way you plan to use your network can help you decide what type of equipment to purchase. A home user who primarily wants the roaming ability of wireless networking has different needs than a person running a small home office. First, you should decide whether to go wireless or wired:

▶ **Wireless for home.** Because the focus of this book is home networking, we tend to favor wireless equipment—it provides ease of setup and freedom to roam about the house (with your laptop, of course) and stay connected to a network. Wireless networks have a set distance over which they can communicate; this distance is the network equipment's *range*. The wireless products we discuss have a maximum range of about 150 feet. (This range can potentially be up to 300 feet, in an unobstructed area, but who lives in a warehouse?) In most cases, you can extend the range of your wireless network by adding an access point, which we explain in Chapter 3, "Installing Hardware." You can also mix wired equipment into your wireless network, for instance, adding a powerline adapter to connect a computer that is out of your access point's range.

▶ **Wired home office.** There are a handful of wired networking possibilities that are designed specifically for home use. Phoneline products, for example, are simple to set up and, often, less expensive than their wireless counterparts. After your equipment is installed, wired and wireless networks work the same way. If you plan to network just a few computers located in the same room, such as in a home office, a wired network might be a better choice.

▶ **On a budget**. A wireless network costs more than its wired counterparts. You can expect to spend about $80 to connect each machine to a wireless network. You can find Ethernet cards for about $20, and cabling isn't pricey. Wireless access points, which allow you to connect wireless network adapters on a network and plug in to broadband modems, are more expensive than wired hubs. Keep in mind that the price of wireless technology continues to fall. The current wireless standard, 802.11b (also called Wi-Fi), will soon be replaced by an even faster standard called 802.11a. This will drive the cost down of earlier wireless networking products. Still, wireless is almost always more expensive than wired options, such as Ethernet, phoneline, and (likely, when it arrives) powerline.

▶ **Broadband for All**. If you are just starting to think about setting up a network, seriously consider connecting it to broadband Internet access, if cable or DSL service is offered in your area. In much of this book, we assume that you want to share fast Internet access, whether you use your network for fun or work. Connecting broadband Internet access makes your network dramatically more useful. You can use your network to download files, pick up e-mail, and browse the Web at far greater speeds than you can with an analog 56 kbps modem.

What You Can Accomplish: Sharing Files, Internet Access, Games, Video, and Music

Now you have a general idea of what you need to start your home network. So, after everything is up and running on your home network, what can you do with it? Here are a few ideas that might help you get more use and enjoyment out of your network.

▶ **Share Internet access**. If you don't want to purchase a router to share Internet access, you can use a built-in feature of Microsoft Windows to do the job. Internet Connection Sharing (ICS) is a feature of Windows 98 Second Edition and later that lets you share a modem with other users on your network. (Chapter 8, "Sharing The Internet," shows you how.)

▶ **Send e-mail and instant messages**. You can communicate with other users on the network.

▶ **Share peripherals**. You probably know that you can connect to any computer on your home network and use any printer as if it were connected to your computer. You can also use the network to back up important files to another computer on the network in case you have a serious PC meltdown.

▶ **Share files**. You can access files and folders on hard drives and CD or DVD drives from any computer in the network. Move an MP3 audio file you downloaded from the Internet on one computer to the only PC in the house with a CD burner.

▶ **Play a game with other folks**. In your house or across the Atlantic, your teammates (and enemies) are no longer dictated by distance.

▶ **Watch a video from a DVD player**. Your kids can watch a DVD upstairs from your laptop downstairs.

▶ **Play MP3s**. Connect to one computer from another and even play MP3 audio files on your home stereo. (See Chapter 6, "Sharing Video and Music," to learn more about wireless technology that can help you do this and eliminate a mess of cables in the process.)

What Now?

In the next chapter, we look at how to lay out your network most effectively. In the meantime, keep a few tips in mind while you decide what kind of network to start. Personally, we prefer to set up a wireless network. There are a few considerations you should keep in mind, though, when considering a wireless network.

▶ A wireless network makes installation simple, but it requires more software configuration. All of the other technologies we discuss in this book use the built-in features of Windows for most networking features, such as file and printer sharing. However, wireless networking equipment usually comes with its own software for additional configuration that other networking hardware does not require.

▶ A wireless network might not be right for every home. Very large homes, or those with steel beams or many walls between one wireless network component (such as a network adapter or access point) and another is not appropriate. The farther away you place a network adapter, the slower it transmits data. Each component can broadcast a signal up to about 150 feet indoors, and about twice that outside. The fewer the obstructions, the better the results for your wireless network.

▶ These wireless cautions aside, in my own home and in offices where I've set up networks, I chose wireless networks. Here's why: You can be up and running quickly, through walls, without using a drill or spending energy running cables. After the network is set up, usually in an afternoon, it usually runs as well as the wired networks I've built. When I don't need to go over a distance of more than 150 feet, I go wireless.

▶ If you have a wireless network at your office and at home, you can use a laptop and a wireless networking card to access both networks. For example, I recommended this setup to my brother, who has a cable modem at home and a DSL modem at work. When he walks in the door of his home or office, his laptop is automatically connected to the wireless network and to the Internet. He's considering moving his office, and if he does, he can easily take his wireless network with him.

Benefits

After you connect your computers together, you'll see some immediate benefits. The benefits are greater if you connect your network to a cable or DSL Internet connection. Most noticeable: You won't need an extra phone line to keep your house busy-signal-free.

▶ **Cost**. You won't need to purchase a printer and modem for each computer in the house.

▶ **Speed**. Sharing a networked, broadband connection is much faster than connecting by a 56 kbps modem at each computer. When you network a broadband Internet connection, everybody gets online whenever they want.

▶ **Access**. Forget about burning CDs and copying files to floppies to transfer files. Say goodbye to SneakerNet. The days of walking a file from one computer to another are over.

2

Laying Out a Network

What hardware do you need to purchase and where does it go? In this chapter, we consider how to design your network. You learn what equipment you need, what bandwidth is, and why it's important.

After you decide what kind of network you want, it's time to figure out where to place your equipment. As the name implies, a hub is the center of most wired networks. We look at installing a hub to expand your setup beyond a two-PC network.

After you've made your hardware choices, we look toward Chapter 3, "Installing Hardware." There, you learn about connecting the hardware you've chosen.

What Is Bandwidth?

Not all networking equipment transfers data at the same speed. When choosing among networking hardware, you should consider bandwidth, the speed at which data travels over your network. Bandwidth is often described in bits per second (bps). A bit is the smallest amount of data a computer can store, a zero or one (see Table 2.1). One alphanumeric character (such as a number, letter, or special character) is made up of eight bits, which equals one byte. The speed of most network equipment is measured in megabits per second (mbps).

Bandwidth is also used to used to describe the speed of different broadband technologies. When talking about Internet connection speed, you'll often hear the word broadband. Broadband usually means Internet connections that transmit data at 1.5 mbps or faster. A digital telephone line called a T-1 can transmit data at up to 1.5 mbps, which makes for a very satisfying, and speedy, Internet browsing experience. T-1 lines are commonly used in office networks.

Many people call cable and DSL home Internet connections broadband, to differentiate these modem connections from the 56 kbps analog modems that work over regular phone lines. Cable and DSL Internet connections offer speeds ranging from about 300 kbps to 1.5 mbps (and sometimes faster).

Table 2.1 Of Bits and Bytes	
Measurement	**What is it?**
Bit	The smallest measurement of storage on a computer; a zero or one. Bits are transferred over a network as pulses of electricity.
Byte	Eight bits. A byte represents one alphanumeric character.
Kilobit	One thousand bits. Most cable and DSL modem connection speeds are measured in kilobits per second (kbps).
Megabit	One million bits. Some fast Internet connections carry data at 1.5 megabits per second (mbps) or faster.

MAXIMUM SPEEDS

For our purposes, bandwidth, data transfer rate, and throughput refer to the same idea: the maximum speed at which data can move across your network.

The Hardware You Need

Ready to start shopping for network equipment? Here's a quick overview of what you need to purchase. This initial equipment gets you started sharing files and printers on your network. Later in the chapter, and in Chapter 8, "Sharing the Internet," we look at adding hardware that lets you share a broadband Internet connection over your network.

For a wireless network, you need:

▶ **A wireless network adapter**. You need a network adapter for each computer in your network. The network adapter transmits data, either to another wireless network card directly, or through a device called an access point (see Figure 2.1), which lets you connect your wireless network to a cable or DSL modem. No matter what kind of wireless network you decide to set up, each computer needs its own network adapter card.

You connect the wireless network card to your computer using the port of your choice. A USB wireless network adapter is typically the easiest to install. To connect a laptop, a PC Card network adapter does the job. You can also install a PCI card into an open slot inside your computer. This is the least attractive option, though, given the extra installation time required to open your computer case. When shopping, keep in mind that some wireless PCI network adapters are really just PC Card adapters. You still need to purchase a PC Card to insert into the PC Card adapter, which is not terribly convenient. Preferably, find a unit that does not require inserting a PC Card and has an antenna for better transmission and reception (see Figure 2.2).

Figure 2.1
A wireless access point lets multiple wireless network adapters, plugged into each of your computers, communicate over radio waves

Figure 2.2
This Linksys PCI
wireless network
adapter includes an
extended antenna
that improves
transmission and
reception of data across
a wireless network
(Photo courtesy of the
Linksys Group, Inc.
2002)

For a wired network, you need:

▶ **Network adapter**. You need a network adapter for each computer in your network.

▶ **Cables**. Phoneline and powerline network hardware plugs into phone jacks and electrical outlets. That's why it's called "no-new-wires" networking. Your house wiring connects one network adapter to another. However, if you choose an Ethernet network, you need to buy enough cable to reach from one computer to another. Most cable used for Ethernet networks is called twisted pair, or Unshielded Twisted Pair (UTP) and resembles regular telephone wiring, but is slightly thicker. In addition, the cable you use for an Ethernet network has eight wires, whereas regular telephone wiring has only four wires inside. The most common cable used for Ethernet networks is called Category 5.

▶ **Hub**. Most wired networks include a hub, but using a hub isn't absolutely necessary. In the next section, we look at expanding your network with a hub.

NETWORK STARTER KIT

Whether you choose to go wireless or wired, you might consider a *network starter kit*. These kits include everything you need to start networking your computers and printers (see Figure 2.3). For a bit more money, you get everything you require for a home network in one box. If you choose to take this route, as your network grows, you can later purchase more network adapters (and cables for a wired network).

Figure 2.3
An Ethernet network kit might be useful if you need to set up a small number of computers

So, should you go wireless or wired? It really depends on how comfortable you are with running wiring in your house and how far the network needs to transfer data.

If you want to use "no new wires" technology, you don't have to go completely wireless. You can use hardware that allows you to connect computers using your existing home phone lines, called HomePNA or simply phoneline. Alternatively, powerline products use your existing home electrical wiring.

No new wires networking hardware is promising because it offers a greater range than wireless networks. In addition, wired products are typically more difficult to hack into, because they don't depend on radio waves, which pass beyond your walls. Table 2.2 shows some of the pros and cons of different network technologies.

CHAPTER 2

Table 2.2
Comparison: Phoneline, Powerline, Wireless, and Ethernet Networks

Network Type	Pros	Cons	Speed	Cost
Phoneline	No additional house wiring required; inexpensive.	You can only connect where you have a phone jack.	10 mbps	About $25 per adapter.
Powerline	Fast; many outlets in any home.	Not widely available.	14 mbps	Because it's the newest technology, it's also the most expensive—about $150 per computer. Prices will fall as the technology matures.
Wireless	Easy to set up; connect anywhere in the home within range (about 150 feet) of a wireless network adapter or access point.	Relatively expensive compared to other networking technologies.	Most wireless equipment, called 802.11b, or Wi-Fi, works at up to 11 mbps. A newer wireless technology, 802.11a, sometimes called Wi-Fi5, works at up to 54 mbps.	About $80 an adapter. You'll spend more for Wi-Fi5 adapters, perhaps twice as much, but prices will drop as the equipment becomes more widespread.
Ethernet	Fast; the least expensive networking technology.	If you need to run cable from one room (or floor) to another, an Ethernet network is more difficult to install than a wireless, phoneline, or powerline network.	Standard Ethernet works at 10 mbps. Fast Ethernet has a maximum bandwidth of 100 mbps.	About $15-20 an adapter.

Expanding Your Network with a Hub

If you need to network more than two computers, you can expand simply and inexpensively using a hub. A hub is usually a square or rounded box into which you plug all the cables connecting your computers. A small, four- or five-port hub is about the size of two packs of playing cards. A hub lets you plug computers and printers into the network and allows data to pass through to each computer on the network simultaneously.

Wired Hubs

If you decide to use Ethernet to create your network, you'll need a hub (see Figure 2.4) to connect three or more computers. You can use hubs to connect other hardware with Ethernet ports as well, such as standalone MP3 players, printers, and devices that allow you to share a printer, called *printer servers*. Some home networking technologies, such as phoneline and powerline, do not require a hub: Your house wiring essentially acts as a hub, allowing you to plug into any phone jack or electrical outlet to share computers.

Figure 2.4
A hub lets you connect multiple computers and printers on your network

If you start shopping around for a hub, you'll soon find yourself asking, "What's the difference between a hub and a switch?" Though they look similar, there is a difference. A hub routes data to all devices without making any distinction about who's supposed to get what. Everybody gets everything. A switch (see Figure 2.5) finds the right destination for the data and handles the job more quickly than a regular hub. Hubs are often used to connect smaller groups of computers within a network, a subnetwork, or to each other. Again, data speed is increased because the switch delivers the data to the intended destination, rather than providing data to every computer on a network. Although hubs are typically less expensive than switches, switches often aren't much more expensive than hubs—so, if you're making the choice between one or the other, buy a switch.

Figure 2.5
A switch is a good bet for large networks and increases the speed of any network—your home network will do fine with a less expensive hub

CHAPTER 2

File and printer sharing won't require the sort of efficiency a switch can provide. Because a switch only sends data to the equipment that is intended to receive it, more bandwidth is available on the network. The result is a more efficient, speedier network. Switches are especially useful when you have individual network segments, groups of computers, or printers networked together. A switch speeds up any network, but you probably won't notice the difference on a home network. An inexpensive hub performs just fine.

CHOOSING A HUB

Look for a hub with more ports than you think you need. You never know when you'll need to add another computer—or printer—to the network. Also, look for a hub with an uplink port (see Figure 2.6), which allows you to connect the hub to another hub (or switch) if you run out of ports. In addition, consider a hub that includes a router, which lets you access the Internet on multiple computers over one Internet connection, and potentially, a firewall, which helps keep unwanted guests off your network. These devices are discussed in Chapter 8, "Sharing the Internet."

Figure 2.6
A hub with an uplink port lets you connect one hub to another, giving you more ports as your network expands

Access Points

In the wireless world, an access point works like a wireless hub, connecting computers in your network. However, access points transmit data using radio waves. In addition to acting as a hub, an access point (sometimes called an AP for short) lets you connect your wireless network to a wired one. A wireless access point might, for extra cost, include a built-in device called a router. A router connects one network to another. If you have a cable or DSL modem, a router connects your network to the Internet and enables you to share Internet access on every computer in your wireless network. If you plan to start a wireless network, seriously consider a wireless access point with a built-in router (see Figure 2.7). You can find a wireless access point, such as those sold by Linksys and Netgear, with a router for between $150-200 on Buy.com or Outpost.com.

Figure 2.7
A Wireless access point
with router (Photo
courtesy of the Linksys
Group, Inc. 2002)

HOW DOES A NETWORK TRANSFER FILES?

Networks transfer files in chunks of data called packets. Packets travel through
the network and are reassembled at their destination. When a hub receives data,
in a form called a data packet, the hub copies the data to all the other ports in
the hub. A data packet is part of a message that includes part of the data being
sent, as well as information on where the data is intended to arrive.

How to Lay Out Your Network (Where to Put Your Equipment)

Building your network takes some consideration, but placing the equipment should be
straightforward.

▶ In a wired network, place your hub where your other equipment, such as
computers and printers, can easily reach it. Most people put their hub in
the center of the network, but you can put it anywhere—as long as you
have enough cable to reach.

▶ In a wireless scenario, placement of your equipment is more important.
Wireless equipment has a maximum range of about 150 feet, sometimes less
in areas with obstructions, including walls, brick, and steel. If you have an
access point, place it as close as possible to the center of the network.

CHAPTER 2

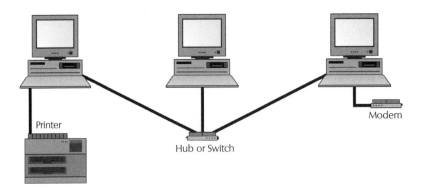

Printer

Hub or Switch

Modem

Wireless networks can work in one of two ways: In a small area, you might do well to use *ad hoc* mode, also called peer-to-peer, which allows the network adapter cards to communicate directly with each other. If you are creating a network that spreads outside of one room, you probably need to purchase an access point, which, as mentioned earlier, works a bit like a wireless hub and allows you to connect a wireless network to a wired network. A wireless network that uses an access point is said to be working in *infrastructure* mode, rather than ad hoc.

COMPATIBILITY AMONG VENDORS

Different pieces of 802.11b wireless networking hardware, sometimes called Wi-Fi or wireless Ethernet, should be compatible. Products that carry the Wi-Fi (short for wireless fidelity) logo are certified by a wireless industry association called the Wireless Ethernet Compatibility Alliance, to work together. That means you can purchase equipment from different manufacturers, and they should still be able to communicate. You could buy a Netgear Wi-Fi (sometimes called 802.11b) access point, and it should work with a 3Com Wi-Fi network adapter.

Network Speed and Internet Access

No matter how fast your network's maximum speed, you are always limited to the speed of the slowest part of your network. Greater bandwidth (higher speeds) means faster Web searches, and pages and e-mail attachments download more quickly. In most cases, the slowest connection is your Internet connection. Your cable modem might be able to download Web pages at 300-700 kbps. Your wireless network speed likely tops out at 11 mbps. If your network is used primarily for Web surfing, just about any network does a fine job of sharing Internet connections.

Most network technologies, such as Ethernet, phoneline, and wireless, transfer data across the network much faster than a cable and DSL modem can access it. Your Web surfing is also limited by how fast the Web server you are downloading from can deliver the page, as well as by the activity of Web-surfing users on your segment of your Internet service provider's network.

DOES SHARING AN INTERNET CONNECTION DECREASE MY SPEED?

When multiple folks in your home use the Internet, it is unlikely that you and the rest of your family will simultaneously download Web pages, audio and video files, or other data. For instance, when you surf a Web page, you click a link, wait for the page to load, then read it. While you're reading, no information is downloading to your hard drive. All the bandwidth your connection can provide is available to everyone else in the house while you are idle. A cable or DSL modem is capable of handling multiple requests from various users over your network with very little noticeable decrease in speed.

Let's look at some typical Internet connection speeds:

▶ **Cable**. Connections typically range in speed from 500 kbps to 1.5 mbps.

▶ **DSL**. Speeds can vary depending on many factors, including how far you are from your phone company's central office, but most companies guarantee DSL speeds of between 128 kbps and 384 kbps (although you might actually see faster speeds).

▶ **Analog modems**. Connections through your telephone line top out at 56 kbps, perhaps much less, depending on the quality of your phone line.

How Hardware Speed Affects Your Network Choices

Of course, speed is not the only consideration when designing your network. In many cases, speed might not be the most important consideration.

You want the fastest possible network hardware when you are transferring files within your own network, from PC to PC. If you do any work with large video clips or database files, or if you produce complex printing jobs, you want as much speed as you can get. In this case, Fast Ethernet is the best choice, with its top speed of 100 mbps.

Wireless networks are the easiest to set up, but wireless networks are limited in bandwidth. The maximum speed of a wireless network is currently 11 mbps, but newer versions of wireless networks produce speeds of up to 45 mbps. However, Fast Ethernet is less expensive and nearly twice as fast as the fastest available wireless network.

The connector you choose for your network adapter is also important. Although USB is convenient for connecting wireless and wired networks to desktop and laptop computers, it does have limitations. USB adapters have a maximum throughput of 12 mbps, which can dramatically reduce the speed of a networking technology like Fast Ethernet.

On a day-to-day basis, most home users won't see a substantial difference from one networking technology to another. But serious gamers and those who routinely transfer large files across the network should look for the fastest hardware they can afford.

Additional Help

For more information on laying out your home network, check out these Web sites. You'll find up-to-date information and tutorials that can help you get started—and stay out of trouble.

► **HomeNetHelp.com (www.homenethelp.com).** Is a site that offers excellent step-by-step tutorials, reviews, and user forums where you can trade stories of setup headaches—and find help—from other networkers like yourself.

► **Practically Networked (www.practicallynetworked.com).** Is another great site for finding help in a pinch. The site has how-to and troubleshooting sections that can help you with installation of wired and wireless networks. Practically Networked also has user forums (you must register first to use them) where you can scratch your head (virtually) with other folks who might have found the solution to your problem.

► **Google Groups (groups.google.com).** Is not network specific, but very helpful—the newsgroup search at Google Groups can be a lifesaver. You can search across many Internet discussion groups for answers to your network installation questions. The groups comp.networks and comp.os.ms-windows.networking.misc are both good places to wander through as you start planning your network.

► **About.com (compnetworking.about.com).** Is known for helping users find information on all sorts of topics. The networking section of the site provides a good jumping off point to additional information. Here, you'll find networking articles, advice, and an extensive collection of links to other helpful networking sites.

3

Installing Hardware

In this chapter, we turn to physically installing different types of networks. What's that you say? You thought you just plugged them in? Well, there's actually a bit more to it than that. But take heart—*connecting* your computers is a relatively straightforward task. Compared to configuring your software, connecting the hardware is the easy part. That said, not all networks are created equal and some take a bit more setup than others. We walk through the steps of setting up wireless, Ethernet, phoneline, and powerline networks.

Getting Started

Ready to plug in your hardware? Here's the basic idea:

▶ Decide what type of network to install (wireless or wired).

▶ If you go wired, decide what kind of hardware to use: Ethernet, phoneline, or powerline.

▶ Choose whether to install PCI, USB, or PC Card network adapters.

▶ Install your network adapters.

▶ Attach cables between your network adapters and your hub. Or, connect computers directly together.

▶ Start your computer.

▶ Share files and printers.

Utility Player: In Praise of USB

A common port found on most computers, USB, works with most types of networking products and can make your life a bit easier. This is especially true if you're not interested in installing hardware inside your computer. Regardless of whether you go wireless or wired, USB can simplify your network setup.

Most USB products require Windows 98 or later (including Windows Me, 2000, or XP). Older Windows 95 computers do not support USB (a later version of Windows 95, called OSR2, does offer USB support). You need to use a PCI or PC Card network adapter, or upgrade to Windows 98 if you want to use USB. For a USB setup, you can choose to install the following network adapters:

▶ **Wireless USB.** Offers freedom from cables and quick set up. One end plugs into an open USB port on your computer. The other end is a radio transmitter/receiver that handles your network communication. (See Figure 3.1.)

▶ **Phoneline USB.** Allows you to use regular phone line wiring to connect your computers, plugged into this network adapter. (See Figure 3.2.)

▶ **Ethernet USB.** Allows you to connect your computer to other computers with Ethernet adapters, broadband modems, and hubs using inexpensive Ethernet cabling. (See Figure 3.3.)

Figure 3.1
A USB wireless network adapter can make installing a network quite simple (Photo courtesy of the Linksys Group, Inc. 2002)

Figure 3.2
A USB phoneline network adapter offers the convenience of using a regular phone jack to get your network started

Figure 3.3
An Ethernet USB adapter can help you connect to an Ethernet network without installing a PCI network card in your computer; the tradeoff? Speed—Ethernet networks max out at 10 or 100 mbps, while USB tops out at 12mbs, plenty for a home network that isn't meant for playing multimedia or very large file transfers

Any of these adapters support the type of data transfer and peripheral and Internet sharing you're likely to need on a home network. If you're short on USB ports, you can purchase a USB hub. Keep in mind, though, that a USB hub is different than a hub used for networking computers, such as an Ethernet hub. You can use an Ethernet hub to run cables from the Ethernet network adapter card to the hub to network your computers. A USB hub provides you with additional ports for your USB computers. But USB networks are used to connect only two computers. Purchasing a USB hub gives you the option to plug in multiple devices, such as a USB printer, scanner, or keyboard. Just plug the hub into an open USB port on your computer.

CHAPTER 3

HOT-SWAPPING EQUIPMENT

USB is handy for another reason. You can "hot-swap" USB equipment, which means that you can plug it in when the computer is on. That said, some networking software does not recognize the network adapter until you first restart the computer. USB isn't the only easy-to-install game in town. PC Card adapters for laptops are also simple to install. However, you must first turn off your computer before you plug in a PC Card. You might crash the computer when you plug in (or eject) a PC Card network adapter while the computer is on. Follow the directions that come with your hardware.

The main drawback of USB is that it won't support the top speed of Fast Ethernet (sometimes called 100BaseT), a version of the Ethernet standard that transmits data at up to 100 mbps. USB has a maximum data rate of 12 mbps. For Internet access, this isn't an issue, because most home broadband connections max out at 1.5 mbps. For playing multiplayer games and transferring large files from one computer to another, you want as much bandwidth as possible. In these instances, USB is not a good fit. In addition, USB adapters are not available for the latest version of wireless networking hardware, 802.11a, which offers a maximum speed of 54mbps.

Starting a Wireless Network

Wiring your house can be a pain (stringing cables around your house, drilling holes in walls, and generally taking years off your marriage). Comparatively, setting up a wireless network is a walk in the park. Here, we walk through a sample installation of a Linksys USB wireless network adapter. When you install a second wireless network adapter, the two adapters can communicate directly with each other, creating a simple wireless network. Once installed, you can share files and printers (see Chapter 5, "Sharing Data and Equipment") and Internet access (see Chapter 8, "Sharing the Internet"). You can expand a wireless network using an access point, which we explain a bit later in this chapter.

Wireless networks work in one of two ways, the pros and cons of which are compared below in Table 3.1:

▶ **Ad-hoc**. Each wireless network adapter communicates directly with another wireless network adapter. You plug an adapter into each computer you want to add to the network. The adapters are radio transmitters and receivers that transmit data over the network; for example, the data can be Web pages you download using a shared cable modem or files you share. An ad-hoc network looks like this:

▶ **Infrastructure**. In this mode, the wireless network adapters do not communicate directly with each other. Instead, all the network adapters communicate with a central wireless hardware device, an access point. An infrastructure network looks like this:

Wireless access point

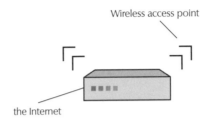

the Internet

Wi-Fi

The most common wireless networking technology is called 802.11b, or Wi-Fi. Wi-Fi transmits data at a maximum of 11 mbps. That's plenty for sharing Internet access and transferring most files. A more recent wireless technology, called 802.11a, or Wi-Fi5, can support speeds of up to 54 mbps. The products aren't widely available yet and pricing is still unclear. You need to choose one or the other—802.11a and 802.11b equipment cannot work together.

Table 3.1
Considering Ad Hoc vs. Infrastructure Wireless Networking

Network Type	Benefits	Drawbacks	Expense
Ad Hoc	Easy to set up; requires no access point.	Limited Range; adding an access point extends your network's range.	About $80 per wireless network adapter.

Table 3.1 (continued)
Considering Ad Hoc vs. Infrastructure Wireless Networking

Network Type	Benefits	Drawbacks	Expense
Infrastructure	Allows you to connect computers farther apart from each other; necessary to share a cable or DSL modem. Note that you can use ad-hoc mode if you configure one PC to share its Internet connection, using Windows Internet Connection Sharing program, and two network adapters: one to connect to the Internet and the other to share access to other computers on the network.	More expensive; takes additional time to configure.	Access points cost between $150-300.

Installing a Simple Peer-To-Peer Wireless Network

Ready to connect? Here's how to get started with a simple 802.11b wireless network.

I tend to favor PC Cards for laptop computers, because they're small and cord-free, and USB for desktops, because they're easy to install. USB has a maximum throughput rate of 12 mbps, and, conveniently, 802.11b (or Wi-Fi) networks operate at a maximum of 11 mbps.

Before you get started installing network adapters, find your Windows operating system disk. Keep that disk handy, because you might be prompted to insert it into your CD drive so that your computer can copy necessary files to your system.

The installation procedure for your wireless network card could vary from the one described here. You might, for instance, need to install your network adapter card before you install your drivers, or vice versa. If so, follow the instructions that came with your equipment. The basic steps, however, should be very similar and you'll quickly see how the process works. You'll be up and running in no time.

1. **Install the network adapter software**. The Linksys USB wireless network adapter requires installation of the bundled software (see Figure 3.4) before attaching the network adapter to the computer. When you finish, turn off the computer.

CHAPTER 3

2. **Install hardware**. Plug the wireless network adapter card into your USB slot on your computer. Turn on the computer.

3. **Install drivers**. When Windows restarts, it recognizes the network adapter. Depending on the version of Windows you are using, you might be prompted for the CD-ROM that comes with the adapter. The disk that comes with your hardware contains the drivers that let Windows recognize the network adapter.

Figure 3.4
The Linksys configuration software for a wireless USB network adapter (Photo courtesy of the Linksys Group, Inc. 2002)

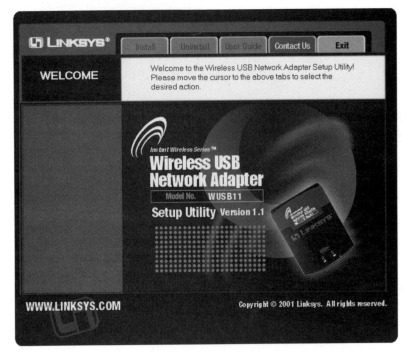

Expand Your Range with a Wireless Access Point

Connecting an access point to your wireless network allows your computers to communicate over a greater distance. You can place your computers farther from each other because each network adapter communicates with a centrally-located access point (see Figure 3.5), rather than with the individual network adapters.

Figure 3.5
A Linksys wireless
access point helps
connect a wireless
network to a wired
network (Photo
courtesy of the Linksys
Group, Inc. 2002)

If your access point is placed as close to the center of your network as you can manage,
you can effectively double the range of your network adapters. For example, two wireless
network adapters can communicate with each other over a range of about 150 feet. Put an
access point in between them, and they can communicate up to 300 feet apart.

In addition to greater range, an access point offers other advantages.

▶ An access point lets you connect your wireless network to a
   broadband modem.

▶ You can connect your access point to an existing, wired network. Say you
   already have some computers networked by Ethernet. You could install
   a wireless network adapter in a laptop, which communicates with the
   access point and connects through an Ethernet port to your Ethernet
   network. You can roam from room to room, using a wireless network
   adapter, and stay in contact with both wired and wireless networked
   computers in your house.

Here's how to get up and running with an access point:

1. Install the configuration software for your access point on one of your
    computers, ideally a laptop. Some access points allow you to connect your
    laptop, using a USB cable, to configure the access point; for instance, to
    enable encryption, and keep potential hackers off your network. In most
    cases, you simply plug in your access point and are ready to go, using
    default settings.

CHAPTER 3

2. Plug your access point into an electrical outlet.

3. Connect through a USB cable and configure the access point. The various settings for your access point are specific to your brand of equipment. In Chapter 10, "Security," we look at encrypting your wireless network to keep unwanted users out.

4. Install your wireless network adapters on the computers you plan to network. You probably need to use the software that came with your network adapter to choose ad-hoc versus infrastructure mode (see Figure 3.6). Remember that infrastructure mode enables your network adapters to communicate through the access point. Ad-hoc mode lets the network adapters communicate directly with each other. Using the wrong setting here can disable your network.

Figure 3.6
Using the configuration software that comes with your wireless network adapter, tell your network adapters to connect to an access point (rather than communicating directly from network adapter to network adapter)—choose Infrastructure, rather than ad-hoc, mode

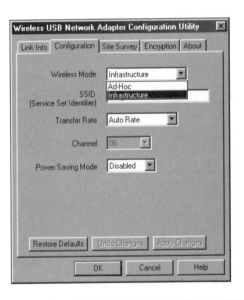

HELP! MY ACCESS POINT STOPPED WORKING!

If your access point appears to stop working and your computers are unable to communicate over the network, you can reset the access point by unplugging it, waiting a few seconds, and plugging it back in. Some access points have a reset button, which has the same effect. It's a quick first step if your wireless network adapters cannot establish a connection to the access point.

Connecting an Ethernet Network

Ethernet networks are so common that if you purchase a new computer, you might already have an Ethernet network adapter installed in it. If you are planning to buy a new computer, consider purchasing a pre-installed Ethernet networking adapter. They're not expensive (usually less than $20) and you won't have to install the card and drivers yourself.

As we mentioned, installing a USB card is a simple plug-and-play operation. Likewise, installing a PC Card connector is straightforward: Plug it in and you're ready to go.

If you do not have a USB port, are using all your USB ports, or need to install a network adapter into a computer using a version of Windows earlier than Windows 98, you might need to install a PCI network adapter card.

Installing a PCI Ethernet Network Card

If you need to install a PCI Ethernet card (see Figure 3.7) into a desktop computer, you'll see that, although not much fun, it isn't terribly difficult. Here's how to do it:

Figure 3.7
A PCI Ethernet card is a solid option for those who don't mind installing a network card into a desktop

1. First, unplug the computer and lift off the computer case.

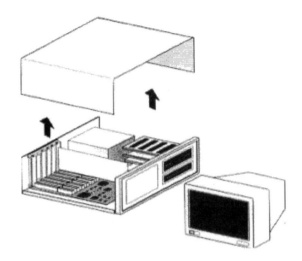

2. Make sure you discharge any static electricity by touching the power supply (a largish metal case near where the electrical plug meets the back of your PC).

3. Find an open PCI slot in your computer.

4. Unscrew the metal back plate that corresponds with the open PCI slot and remove it.

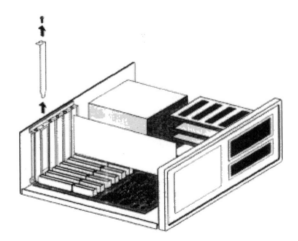

5. Insert the card until it clicks in.

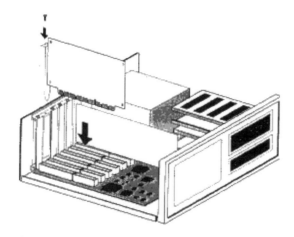

6. Put the case back on the computer and plug it in.
7. Reboot the computer and install the driver. (See Figure 3.8.)

Figure 3.8
Install the driver

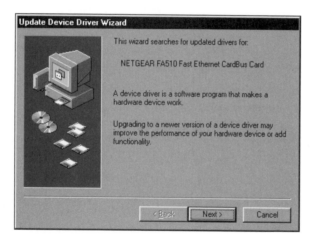

DRIVER VERSIONS

When installing a new network card, make sure you have the latest drivers from the manufacturer's Web site. If your network is running correctly, don't bother installing a new driver. If you are starting a new network, the latest driver can sometimes help correct connection hang-ups. Some common NIC manufacturers and their download sites include:

3Com—www.3com.com support.3com.com

D-Link—www.dlink.com/tech/

Linksys—www.linksys.com/download/

Proxim—www.proxim.com/support/software/

Netgear—support1.netgear.com/netgear1/

Intel—support.intel.com

Compaq—www.compaq.com/support/files/networking/

A Few Words on Cables

When purchasing wiring, look for inexpensive Unshielded Twisted Pair (UTP) cable, which resembles phone wiring. Also, use Category 5 (rather than Category 3) cable, which supports Fast Ethernet, a.k.a. 100BaseT. You can purchase Category 3 cable, for a bit less money perhaps, but it supports only 10BaseT, which tops out at 10 mbps rather than 100 mbps. Okay, now we've just thrown a lot of detail at you, which you probably won't need. Just look for Ethernet patch cables, in the length you need, and you'll be all set.

In addition, avoid coaxial cable. Coaxial cable is thicker than UTP, and it looks just like the wiring used to connect your cable TV box to your television. Coaxial cable is often used to connect one computer directly to another, without the use of a hub. Stick with UTP, which is typically less expensive. A hundred meters is the maximum length for 10BaseT or 100BaseT cable.

In general, when purchasing Ethernet hubs, a 10BaseT Ethernet device performs fine for most home networking needs. If you use Category 5 cable, you can upgrade to 100BaseT later if you decide you need more bandwidth from your network. *Autonegotiating* hubs and network adapters are another option: They can transmit data at either 10 mbps or 100 mbps.

Connecting an Ethernet Hub

To add an Ethernet hub to your network, you need one with enough available ports (probably 4, 8, or 12) and a cable for every computer you want to connect. Cables you purchase with RJ-45 connectors (slightly larger than telephone connectors) on each end are sometimes called patch cables. Here's how to get connected:

1. Connect one end of a patch cable into the hub.
2. Connect the other end of the cable into the network adapter in your PC.
3. Restart your computer.

Most hubs and network adapters have a green light that glows when you are correctly connected. You should see a green light on both your hub and adapter. If your adapter's green light does not glow, try reinstalling the driver.

Connecting through Outlets and Phone Jacks

Speedy powerline products that plug into your home electrical outlets are now available, carrying network data at up to 14 mbps. Early powerline products upset users with slow speeds (about 350 kbps) and line noise from the electrical wiring that made data transfer unpredictable.

Powerline networking products are promoted by the HomePlug Powerline Association (www.homeplug.org). Products using the new faster standard were planned for release in March 2002.

More commonly used are phoneline products, sometimes called HomePNA, a phoneline networking standard promoted by an industry association called the Home Phoneline Network Alliance. HomePNA uses regular phone connectors (RJ-11) and shares phone lines with your telephones without disrupting your phone calls. You can purchase a two-PC phoneline networking kit for about $50 (see Figure 3.9).

Figure 3.9
A phoneline
networking kit
provides everything
you need to get two
PCs connected

Connecting a Phoneline Network

Plugging in a phoneline network is as simple as connecting an Ethernet network.

1. Install the network adapter card on the computer you want to network. Start your computer.

2. When Windows starts up, install drivers from the CD that comes with your network adapter.

3. Plug the phone cable into the phoneline network adapter and the other end into a regular telephone (RJ-11) wall jack.

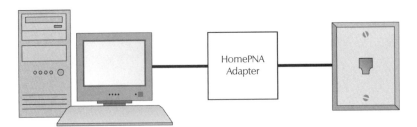

Connecting a Powerline Network

Recently, I tested a handful of new home networking products, including some pre-release powerline hardware. The technology is impressive, both speedy and easy to install. What's the catch? Price. Powerline products tend to be nearly twice as expensive as 802.11b (Wi-Fi) products.

Here's how to get going with a powerline network.

1. Plug in your powerline adapter. You can connect by USB port, or you can use a powerline Ethernet bridge, which plugs into your Ethernet network card (if you have one).

2. Start your computer. If you have a USB network card, install the drivers. The powerline Ethernet bridge does not require you to install new drivers.

3. If prompted to restart your computer, do so. After restarting, you should be all set.

Networking PCs and Macs

There are a handful of ways to network PCs and Macs. You can share files, and printers, between computers using the two operating systems, with one catch. You probably need to purchase and install some software to get the job done.

The program Dave, from Thursby Software, and PCMACLAN from Miramar Systems, are two popular programs for making PCs and Macs get along. Both programs cost less than $150 for a single copy. You either install the software on one or more Macs (as with Dave) or one or more PCs (as with PCMACLAN). You won't have to install the software on both operating systems.

SHARING FILES BETWEEN MACs AND PCs

If you only occasionally need to transfer files between Macs and PCs, you can, of course, simply e-mail a file from one computer to another. Another quick fix: Upload (copy) files from your computer to a server on the Web. You can use a program like WS_FTP (www.ipswitch.com) for PCs or Fetch (www.fetchsoftworks.com) for Macs, to upload files to a server. Often, the Internet Service Provider (ISP) that provides your dial-up Internet service also offers some free space where you can upload (and download) files. Potentially, you can run your own Web server on your machine. You can install the Microsoft Personal Web Server from the Windows 98 CD (or download it from http://www.microsoft.com/msdownload/ntoptionpack/askwiz.asp). On Mac OS 8 and later, under Control Panels, you can use the applet called Web Sharing.

You can find more about the products here:

▶ PC MACLAN (www.miramarsys.com)
▶ Dave (www.thursby.com)

Often, you need to network one computer using a particular operating system onto a group of multiple computers using another operating system (a Mac on a network of PCs, for instance). Use PC MACLAN if you need to get a PC sharing files on a network of Macs, and use Dave if you want to share files from a Mac on a network of PCs.

Assume, for instance, that your significant other, a Mac user, wants to print and share files from your networked PCs. Install Dave on each Mac that needs to share files (see Figure 3.10). Keep in mind that you must purchase a copy of Dave for each Mac that you want to put on the network.

You can use these programs over wired and wireless networks. One approach might be to use the Apple AirPort, an 802.11b hub and router, to network your Macs and PCs. You need an AirPort card for each Mac and an 801.11b network adapter for each PC.

Figure 3.10
Installing Dave on a
Mac to share files on a
PC network

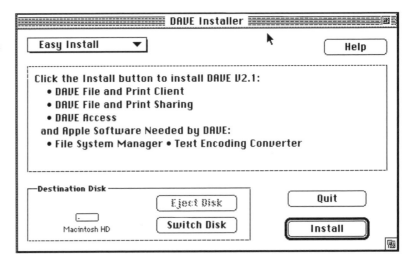

DIGGING DEEPER: MACs AND PCs

For more complex jobs, check out the MacWindows Web site: http://www.macwindows.com. The site offers tips for getting all flavors of Macs and Windows talking to each other.

Another good site that can help you with Macs and PCs: www.homepcnetwork.com/

If the idea of working with a wireless Apple AirPort network appeals to you, check out:

http://www.apple.com/airport/

You can also find good ideas on AirPort networks from this online user forum:

http://discussions.info.apple.com/

4

Direct Connections

In this chapter, we consider how to create a simple network connection when you need to move files or upgrade your computer. Because not everyone needs to network multiple computers in different rooms of the house, knowing how to set up a quick network for a simple file-sharing arrangement can be pretty handy.

Direct connections can be used to connect two PCs on a network or to give a computer that's not on the network access to the network. You can use a parallel, serial, USB, or Ethernet cable, or even connect wirelessly (if both your computers have infrared ports—most laptops do, but most desktops do not).

These tips are especially useful for laptops or when you need to connect to a computer— often a laptop—temporarily. Even if you already have a network, it's good to know how to get two PCs talking directly for unexpected situations. Direct connections come in handy, especially when you want to help a non-networked family member transfer files from an old computer to a new one.

A cable connection is also a good way to network quickly and inexpensively. That said, for the effort it takes to get a cable connection going—especially if you plan to use this setup frequently—consider setting up a regular network. (See Chapter 2, "Laying Out a Network" and Chapter 3, "Installing Hardware.")

Using an Ethernet Crossover Cable to Share Files

If you want to connect only two computers (and you don't have a hub), you need to use a special cable called a crossover cable. If both computers you want to connect have Ethernet network adapters, you can plug in a crossover cable to directly network the two computers. If you try to use a regular Ethernet cable (sometimes called a straight-through or patch cable) to connect two computers, it won't work. In addition, you might need a crossover cable to connect your broadband modem to a router, depending on how your modem's Ethernet port is wired. It's a good idea to read your modem's manual to see if you need a crossover or straight-through cable. One way to verify you are using the correct cable is to look for the green Link light on your network adapter, modem, and hub. The green Link light won't be illuminated if you're using the wrong cable.

A crossover cable is a cable with its transmit and receive pins reversed. There are eight wires and eight pins inside a normal Ethernet 10BaseT cable. Four wires are used: Two wires send data and two receive. They send data directly to the corresponding pins on the other side of the cable. Pins 1 and 2 transmit, and pins 3 and 6 receive.

Here's an inside view of how a normal twisted-pair cable for an Ethernet network is wired:

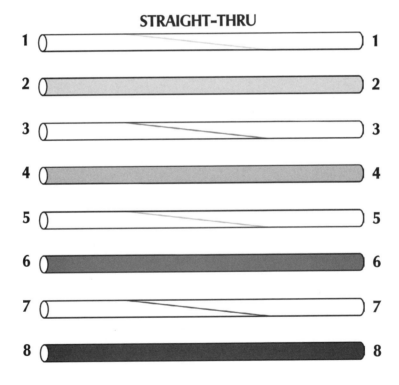

STRAIGHT-THRU

You can see that the wires pass through directly. That's why a regular cable is sometimes called a straight-through cable.

On a crossover cable, pins 1 and 2 connect to 3 and 6. Pins 3 and 6 connect to 1 and 2. The inside of a crossover cable looks like this:

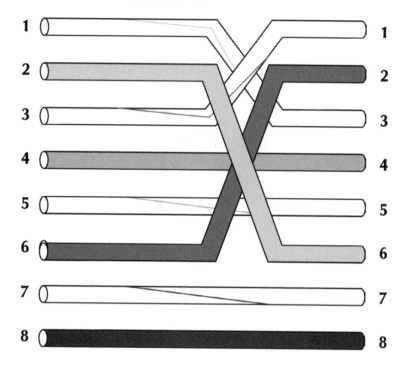

A crossover cable appears just like a normal cable, on the outside. The main difference you'll notice when shopping for a crossover cable is the price. Crossover cables are more expensive than patch cables.

Note that you can't use a crossover cable to connect a PC to a hub, and you can't use a straight-through cable to connect (only) two computers together. Computers connect to a hub using straight-through cables. A hub is your best choice for connecting two or more computers, as it tends to create a more reliable connection than a crossover cable. But when you have no hub, a crossover cable can be a really handy way to get two computers talking.

CONNECTING HUBS
Crossover cables are sometimes used to connect two hubs together. Check with your hub manufacturer to see what kind of cable you need. Some hubs come with a feature that lets you use regular straight-through cables, which are less expensive, to connect hubs. It depends on how the Ethernet port on your peripheral is wired.

Making a Direct Cable Connection

Setting up a quick network really isn't that hard. But if you need to make a temporary connection between a couple of computers, and you don't need all the flexibility, speed, and reliability of a network, try a direct cable connection. Windows is set up to handle direct cable connections without having to install additional software. To see if you have the Direct Cable Connection feature installed, click the Start button and then look under Programs > Accessories > Communication. If you don't see it, don't worry. We'll install it later in the chapter. (See the section "Using the Direct Cable Connection Applet.")

You can use parallel and serial cables (as well as an infrared wireless connection) to transfer files from one PC to another using a direct cable connection. Note that you need a special cable to do the job. You need a cable that is specifically wired to connect two PCs directly together, whether the cable is USB, parallel, or serial.

Windows does not offer a feature to transfer files from one computer to another using a USB cable. This is unfortunate, as USB cables are much faster than parallel and serial cables (see Table 4.1). If you want to connect computers using USB, you need to install special software, which we'll look at later in the chapter.

Table 4.1 Cable Speed Comparison	
Cable	**Maximum Speed (Note: Eight bits equals one byte.)**
USB	12 mbps (megabits per second)
Parallel	115 KBps (kilobytes per second)
Serial	115 kbps (kilobits per second)

WHERE TO PURCHASE CABLES

You can purchase most types of cables for direct connections at an electronics store, such as Best Buy or Circuit City (check your regional equivalent). Just make sure you buy a cable for direct connections, rather than a cable for connecting your printer or modem, which won't work. If you aren't in a big rush, you can purchase cables online and have them delivered to you. A popular online seller is Parallel Technologies: www.lpt.com.

Connecting with a Parallel Cable

Direct connection parallel cables are the most likely way to connect two computers together if you don't have a network interface card in each computer. For instance, if you need to connect a laptop to another computer to trade a few files, a parallel port can do the job. The parallel port on your computer transfers data faster than the serial ports, and it's typically used to connect your computer to a printer. However, a printer cable won't work for file transfers. You need a parallel cable that is specifically made for file transfers. See the previous tip for obtaining the cable you need.

USB IN YOUR FUTURE

USB will likely replace serial and parallel ports on PCs in the next few years. USB connections are much faster and can support 127 peripherals connected (or *daisy chained*) at one time.

Connecting with a Serial Cable

You are probably used to seeing a serial port on the back of your computer—it's used for connecting your modem and, in some cases, your mouse. A connection made through a serial port is slower than a parallel cable connection, but a serial port may be your only open port, and it still gets the job done. (See Figures 4.1a and 4.2b.)

Figure 4.1a
A serial cable, called a null modem cable, can be used to transfer files from one computer to another

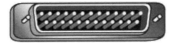

Figure 4.1b
A parallel cable can be used for direct cable connections between (only) two computers and is faster than serial connections

A.K.A.

Serial ports are sometimes called RS-232 ports or COM (communication) ports.

In general, if you have a free parallel port, use a parallel cable. Remember when I said that Windows can't make direct connections over USB? There is a way around this limitation of Windows. USB is faster than serial and parallel, but you need special software to use it. If you have a USB port open, and software, such as LapLink or Symantec's pcAnywhere, use USB. If you have only a free serial port, you need to purchase a null-modem serial cable. Of course, keep in mind that if you want to save yourself the expense and setup time of using a serial connection, you might consider transferring the files by e-mail instead.

After you have your parallel or serial cable connected to both computers, the steps for setting up the direct cable connection are the same. We walk through them in the next section.

FOR SMALLER JOBS

If you want to save yourself the expense and setup time of using a serial connection, transferring the files by e-mail might be a better option for a small job.

Using the Direct Cable Connection Applet

Most Windows installations already have the Direct Cable Connection program installed, but if your computer doesn't have it, you can install it using the Windows Add/Remove Programs applet. Get started by putting your Windows disk in your CD-ROM drive.

1. Select Start > Settings > Control Panel. Double-click Add/Remove Programs.
2. Click the Windows Setup tab. Double-click Communications.
3. Select Direct Cable Connection and click OK. (See Figure 4.2.)

Figure 4.2
If it's not already
installed, you need to
add Direct Cable
Connection to your
computer if you want
to trade files using this
program

How to Establish a Connection

Starting a direct cable connection is straightforward. The Direct Cable Connection wizard
steps you through identifying the host computer, which has the files you want to access.
Then, you identify the other computer as the guest. Afterward, you choose which port
you'll use to transfer data, an available parallel or serial port.

If File and Printer Sharing has not been set up on the host computer, you need to do so
and then reboot. You should also make sure that a folder or drive is shared before you
attempt to make a direct cable connection. For instructions on how to set up File and
Printer Sharing, see Chapter 5, "Sharing Data and Equipment." After you make the direct
cable connection, you can view the host computer's shared folder (or drive) on the guest
computer.

1. From the computer with the files you want to access, select Start >
   Programs > Accessories > Communications.

2. Choose Direct Cable Connection.

3. The Direct Cable Connection wizard asks you whether you want to act
   as the host or guest (see Figure 4.3). Select Host. A dialog box appears
   that tells you the host computer is waiting for a guest computer to
   connect (see Figure 4.4).

4. Follow these steps again from the computer onto which you will be copying the files, but select Guest (instead of Host) in Step 3.

Figure 4.3
The Direct Cable Connection applet walks you through connecting to another computer

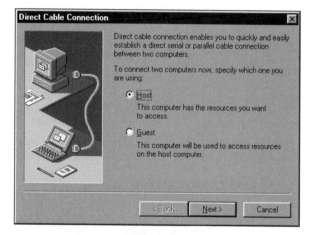

Figure 4.4
The Host computer waits for the Guest computer to connect

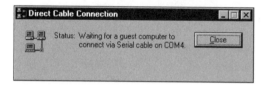

THE DIRECT CABLE CONNECTION WIZARD
The wizard menu only shows up the first time you connect. After that, the connection is made automatically when you start the Direct Cable Connection program.

Connecting with Infrared

You can also use infrared to transfer files. Many notebook computers, but not all, have infrared ports built in, which are useful for wireless file transfers.

Infrared is an invisible beam of light and is used in laptops, PDAs, TV remote controls, and stereos. Infrared is a line-of-sight technology, which means that you need to line up the infrared ports on the two computers without any obstructions between them.

Here's how to connect directly using infrared:

1. Many laptops offer infrared capability, but most desktops do not. To enable infrared capability, select Start > Settings > Control Panel and double-click Infrared.

2. Click the Options tab and choose Enable infrared communication. Note the ports on which infrared will be enabled (see Figure 4.5).

3. Select Start > Programs > Accessories > Communications.

4. Select Direct Cable Connection.

5. The Direct Cable Connection wizard appears (as shown in Figure 4.6).

6. You are asked what port you want to use. Choose the port that Windows enabled in Step 1.

Figure 4.5
Enable infrared
communication

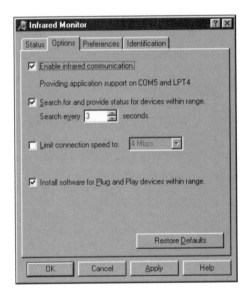

Figure 4.6
Start an infrared
connection between
two computers

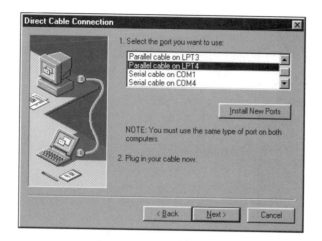

CHAPTER 4

Speed Issues with Direct Cable Connections

USB is the easiest/fastest way to quickly transfer files, but Direct Cable Connection doesn't offer USB as an option. Compared to most home networking technologies, parallel and serial connections are very slow and allow you to connect a maximum of only two computers.

Obviously, a traditional network is both much faster (consider an Ethernet network running at 10-100 mbps) and easier to use on a day to day basis.

If you only occasionally need to connect a computer to your network, consider a USB or PC Card network adapter for just about any kind of network (Ethernet, wireless, or phoneline). You can easily use a USB or PC Card network adapter as you need it and plug it into another machine when one machine isn't being used on the network.

Using USB

USB should be one of the simplest (and fastest) ways to make a direct connection. However, connecting through USB works slightly differently than connecting with the other common cables mentioned previously. You need a program that offers USB support for transferring files, such as LapLink (see Figure 4.7) or Symantec's pcAnywhere. You can find more about the software at the companies' Web sites: www.laplink.com and www.symantec.com.

Figure 4.7
LapLink lets you use a USB connection to transfer files

You need a special kind of USB cable to make the connection. Again, you can purchase the necessary cables at Parallel Technologies (www.lpt.com). The site also offers advice and software for making direct connections. The program you use for USB-based file transfer might come bundled with the appropriate USB cable. Ask to make sure before purchasing.

In addition to offering file transfer, LapLink and pcAnywhere let you remotely control a computer, over a network connection, just as if you were sitting in front of the PC. You can access the computer you want to remotely control over the Internet, using a serial, parallel, or USB cable, or you can call the computer directly using a modem.

This arrangement can be really handy when you leave a file at home or in the office. You can dial in over the Internet, from work, or use a modem connection from your laptop. You can dial the computer directly or make a connection over the Internet.

We discuss using both programs for remote control in Chapter 9, "Remote Access."

Transfer Files with Windows Messenger

In some cases, the simplest way to transfer files when you don't have a permanent network is to use the Internet. You can use Windows Messenger, which is bundled with Windows XP, to trade files. Here's how:

1. Launch Windows Messenger.
2. Select the contact to whom you will transfer a file (see Figure 4.8).
3. Select File > Send a file.
4. Browse to the file you want to send and click Open (as shown in Figure 4.9). The file is sent.

Figure 4.8
Windows Messenger offers another handy way to trade files from one computer to another, over the Internet or over your network—choose the contact who should receive the file

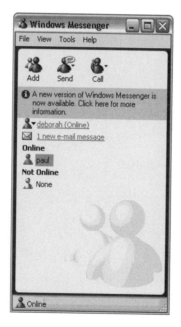

Figure 4.9
Select the file and click
Open—that's all there
is to it

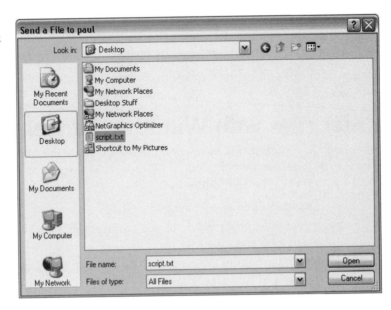

5

Sharing Data and Equipment

In this chapter, we look at two of the tasks you'll perform most frequently after your network is up and running: file and printer sharing. You learn how to how to set up Windows to provide access to files and equipment on the network.

We make a few assumptions—essentially that you've connected your hardware, as we've gone over in the last few chapters. A quick review:

If you are setting up a wireless network:

▶ Each of your computers has a wireless network card installed (along with the software that came with it).

▶ Your computers communicate directly with each other in *ad-hoc* mode or, instead, communicate with an access point in *infrastructure* mode. See Chapter 3, "Installing Hardware," for more information.

If you are setting up an Ethernet network:

▶ Your network interface cards are installed.

▶ If you are connecting three or more computers, they are each connected by cable to a hub. Or, if you are connecting just two computers, you are using a crossover cable. See Chapter 4, "Direct Connections," for more details.

If you are setting up a phoneline or powerline network:

▶ Your hardware is installed.

▶ Each computer is plugged into a phone or power jack.

Your hardware manufacturer may have already set up your computers to share files and printers. If not, a Windows computer typically has the Windows Client for Networking installed, which allows you to share printers and files, once you tell Windows to do so. Here's how.

Naming a Computer

It's the big day. Time to stop calling your computer "laptop" or "Toshiba" and give it a name you can remember. Each computer on your Windows network needs a unique name and needs to be associated with what Windows calls a *workgroup*. You can have multiple workgroups on your network, but in a home with a few computers, one workgroup certainly does the job.

Naming a computer is straightforward enough. The computer and workgroup names should be no longer than fifteen characters (see Figure 5.1). The workgroup is comprised of the computers you see when you double-click the Network Neighborhood icon on your desktop.

Figure 5.1
Each computer on your network needs a unique name and you also need a workgroup name

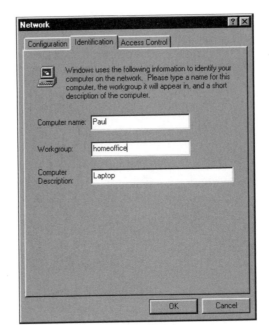

1.   Right-click the Network Neighborhood icon on your desktop.

2.   Select Properties.

3.   Click the Identification tab.

4.   Enter a computer name and workgroup name. Then click OK. Add a description, which other users on the network will see when they open up Network Neighborhood on their desktops.

AN ALTERNATIVE ROUTE
You can also open the Network dialog box (to name your computer or make other changes to your network) by selecting Start > Settings > Control Panel > Network.

Set Up File and Printer Sharing

The meat and potatoes of any network is the capability to share your files and printers. After your network hardware is connected, you should become familiar with the Network Neighborhood icon on your desktop (or the My Network Places icon in Windows Me, 2000, and XP).

To Start Sharing Files in Windows 95/98

To enable File and Print Sharing on Windows 95/98 systems, you should:

1. Right-click the Network Neighborhood icon on your desktop.
2. Select Properties from the shortcut menu that appears.
3. The Network dialog box opens (as shown in Figure 5.2).

Figure 5.2
The Network
dialog box

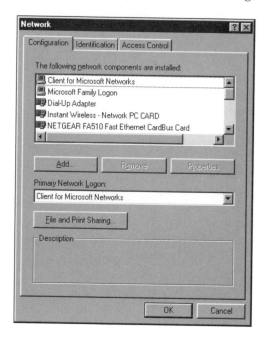

4. Click the File and Print Sharing button.

5. Select "I want to be able to give others access to my files" and "I want to be able to allow others to print to my printer(s)." (See Figure 5.3.) Don't check the printer box if you won't be sharing a printer on this PC.

Figure 5.3
Click the File and Print Sharing button to open the File and Print Sharing dialog box

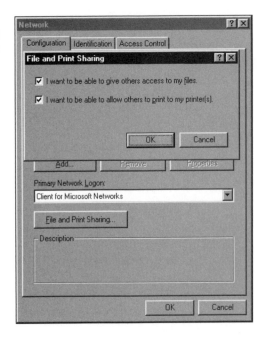

NETWORK NEIGHBORHOOD ICON
You can also reach Network Neighborhood by opening Windows Explorer and, under the Desktop area, selecting the Network Neighborhood icon.

Share a Folder

Sharing a folder on your hard drive is easy business. After the folder is made available on the network, all the folders inside the main folder are also available on the network.

A.K.A.

Sometimes folders on your computers are called directories.

Sharing Folders in Windows 95/98

1. Double-click the My Computer icon on your desktop and navigate to the folder you want to share. Right-click the folder and select Sharing (as shown in Figure 5.4).

2. Select the Sharing tab.

3. Select the Shared As radio button.

4. Choose whether to require a password (see Figure 5.5). This step leaves a lot to your discretion. On a network that isn't connected to the Internet, you shouldn't have to worry much about passwords. However, on a connection that is connected full-time to the Internet, such as a cable or DSL connection, requiring a password to access files on your hard drive makes good sense. Keep in mind that when you share a directory, all of its subdirectories are made available too.

Figure 5.4
Right-click the folder you want to make available on the network and choose Sharing

Figure 5.5
If you want to protect a folder, you should require a password

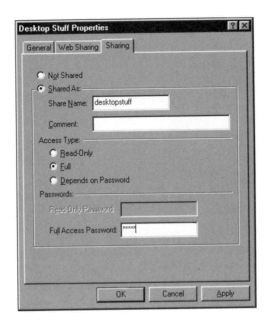

Sharing Folders in Windows XP

You must identify which folders will be shared (and thus accessible) on your network. If you are using Windows XP, you should:

1. Right-click the folder.
2. Select Sharing and Security....
3. Select the Sharing tab.
4. Select the box marked "Share this folder on the network" (see Figure 5.6) and enter a Share name.

Sharing Folders on a Mac

Folks with Macs are used to built-in networking features that have been around since the first Macs were introduced. Here's how to share files on a Mac (OS 9):

1. Choose File Sharing, from the Apple menu.
2. Under the File Sharing section of the Control Panel, choose Start.
3. Close the dialog box.
4. Share a file or folder by selecting it; choose File, Show Info (Command+i).

You can find tutorials and advice on Mac networking online at the excellent Threemacs.com Web site.

Figure 5.6
Sharing a folder in
Windows XP

CHAPTER 5

Using Network Neighborhood

Network Neighborhood, like My Computer, is a handy tool for finding your way around your (networked) computer. If you've been wondering what that icon is for, you're about to find out. Depending on how you open Network Neighborhood (double-clicking to see computers on your network, or right-clicking to view your network properties) you can learn a lot about how your network works (and make changes when necessary).

To see what printers and folders are available on your network:

1. Double-click Network Neighborhood. The Network Neighborhood dialog box opens, as shown in Figure 5.7.

2. To see computers outside your workgroup, double-click Entire Network.

3. To see the folders and printers a computer is sharing, double-click the computer's icon.

Figure 5.7
Opening up Network
Neighborhood to see
the shared computers
on the network

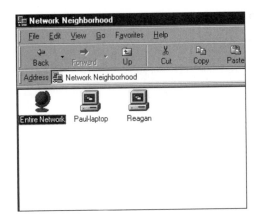

COOL TOOLS

You can see the computers connected to your network by clicking Start > Programs > Accessories > System Tools > Net Watcher. When a user opens a shared file or folder on your system, Net Watcher shows you who's connected to your computer, and for how long. You can also unceremoniously give somebody the boot, by clicking the Disconnect user button. Just make sure they're not writing a file to your drive at that time, or you risk data loss. You can send messages between computers on your network by opening WinPopup. Click Start > Run and type in Winpopup. Each user who wants to send and receive messages needs to run Winpopup.

Sharing a Printer

Sharing a printer takes just a few minutes. Set it up once and you shouldn't have to worry about it again. After you share a printer on your network, anyone on the network can use it.

The directions differ only slightly for Windows 95 and Windows XP. We give the directions for Windows 98 and XP, but if you get the general idea, you'll have no problem sharing a printer on any Windows computer.

1. Open the Control Panel and select Printers (or Printers and Faxes in Windows XP).

2. Right-click the Printer you want to share and choose Sharing (as shown in Figure 5.8).

3. Select "Shared As" or, in XP, "Share this printer."

Figure 5.8
Right-click the printer
you want to share

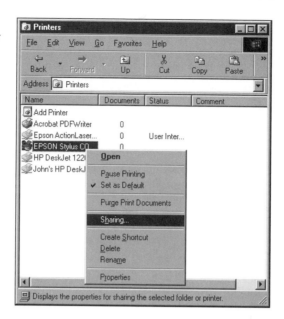

To use a shared printer on your PC, you need to first add the printer to your system (Windows sometimes calls this "installing" a printer). You can select the shared printer from Network Neighborhood and choose File > Install. Then follow the Add Printer wizard's directions. Here's another way to add a printer that's shared on the network:

1. Open Network Neighborhood from your desktop.
2. Choose the computer with the printer you want to install.
3. Double-click the printer's icon.
4. The Add Printer wizard appears and walks you through installation of the printer's drivers on your system. (See Figure 5.9.)

Figure 5.9
Install a shared printer
on the computer
you're using

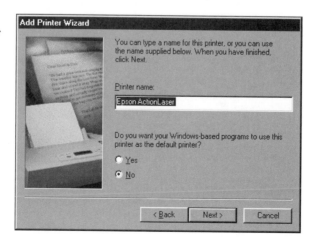

PRINTING TIP

Once you install the shared printer on your computer, you can print to it from within any of your applications, just as you would if it were attached to your computer.

Mac users can share printers using built-in features of the operating system. You can share LocalTalk, Ethernet, and USB printers, though each is set up differently. The steps for each are beyond the scope of this book, but here's how to share a USB printer over a network:

1. From the computer which has the printer attached, open the USB Printer Sharing control panel.

2. Click the Start button.

3. You can print to the printer by opening the USB Printer Sharing control panel.

4. Click the Add button and choose the shared printer you want to use.

Sharing Your Hard Drive or CD-ROM

You can share an entire hard drive (if you don't mind all the subdirectories being shared too) or CD-ROM or DVD drive. The process works much as it does when sharing a folder:

1. Double-click the My Computer icon to see the drive you want to share.

2. Right-click the drive and choose Sharing (as shown in Figure 5.10).

3. Just as you would with a folder, click Share As, enter a name, and decide whether a password is necessary to use the drive.

4. Click OK. The drive is now available on your network.

Figure 5.10
Share a CD-ROM drive with everyone on the network—a handy way to install software over the network

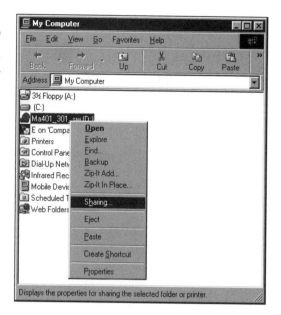

Mapping a Network Drive

You can create a sort of shortcut to a network folder or drive by *mapping* a network drive. Mapping a network drive simply means giving directories shared on your network a letter designation so that you can access them more easily (for instance, your primary hard drive is usually drive "C"). Mapping a network drive isn't necessary, but it gives you faster access to your shared network resources, including folders you use often and CD-ROM drives.

Mapping a network drive also makes the directory appear in My Computer, just as if it were an actual drive on your system. You can then access the drive more easily. Here's how to set it up:

1. Double-click the Network Neighborhood icon (or My Network Places for Windows Me, 2000, or XP).

2. Right-click the shared folder or drive you want to map and select "Map Network Drive."

3. Click Share As, enter a name, and decide whether a password is necessary to use the drive.

4. Click OK. The drive is now available on your network.

CHAPTER 5

Figure 5.11
Assign a drive letter to the network computer or directory you want to share

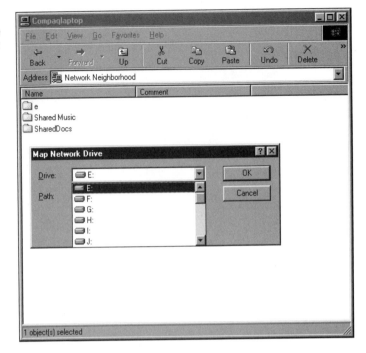

If you later decide to disconnect the drive, right-click the drive (from My Computer) and select "Disconnect."

DISCONNECT A NETWORK DRIVE
You can also disconnect a network drive from Windows Explorer. Click the Tools menu, then select Disconnect Network Drive. Choose the drive you want to disconnect and then click the OK button. Or, right-click Network Neighborhood and choose Disconnect Network Drive.

Sharing Other Peripherals

On your home network, some peripherals are easier to access than others: A printer and hard drive are simple to use—a scanner or digital camera is a bit more awkward.

You might want to share a scanner between two computers in the same room, for instance. Some companies, including Hewlett Packard and Umax, make scanners that can be controlled from any computer over the network. Some of these scanners are quite expensive and are more appropriate for an office environment.

The simplest—and least costly—solution to sharing a scanner or digital camera is to simply share the directory where images are saved from your camera or scanner. For example, scan at the computer where the scanner is connected, then save your images on the network so that everyone can access them.

1. Scan your image.

2. Save the image to a folder.

3. Share the folder.

Likewise, you can share files from your digital camera over the network. Just save the image files from your digital camera to a folder on the computer where the camera is connected. Then share the folder.

CHAPTER 5

6

Sharing Video and Music

After the getting-down-to-brass tacks approach of the last few chapters, we can now begin to have some fun with your new hardware. A home network can be a great way to enjoy music and video all over your house and greatly add to your enjoyment of your computers.

Multimedia over a home network, however, isn't all gravy. Most networking technology was developed decades ago to deliver information in a way that wouldn't lose data. Priority was not given to developing a protocol in which, say, audio and video data traveled from computer to computer in an uninterrupted data stream; it just needed to arrive at its intended destination. Hence, playback can be a little spotty, with gaps in music and jerky motion in video.

That said, if you pick out your equipment with a little prior knowledge, you can avoid these problems. Certain networks are better capable of handling multimedia than others. And surprisingly, the fastest network is not always the best for enjoying audio and video. We consider the best technology for:

▶ Listening to MP3 files from one computer to another

▶ Playing audio from your computer (from a CD or MP3) on your stereo

▶ Watching video from one computer on another elsewhere in the house

What Kind of Multimedia You Can Share

You can share video and audio over your network, including some pretty cool stuff you can find on the Web. Here's a quick look at the types of files you might want to access over your home network:

▶ **Web video**. Home networks are a great way to view videos you download from the Internet. You can download and watch movie trailers, music videos, film shorts, and all sorts of other video from the Web. See www.apple.com/quicktime for trailers, and www.launch.com for music videos. Audio and video files are typically in one of several popular file types. Apple offers QuickTime, a high-quality video file format. RealNetworks offers the Real format, which is often used to both listen to audio and watch video over the Web (Figure 6.1). Another format is MPEG, a way of compressing a video file to reduce its size and make it more appropriate for download over the Internet. These are the most popular formats for watching video on the Web.

▶ **MP3 audio**. You can double-click a song located on one computer and hear it on another. Some networks, such as phoneline or 802.11a, offer consistently higher speeds than others, such as 802.11b. However, most networks should adequately handle MP3 audio.

▶ **Video from a camera**. You can connect cameras, some wireless, that send video over the network. D-Link, for example, makes a wireless 802.11b camera that can be placed anywhere in a house. These cameras can be useful for home security, keeping an eye on a baby, or for communicating through video chat.

▶ **Full-screen DVD**. The promise of being able to watch full-screen video from one computer on another is one of the most exciting future possibilities of home networking. However, video files are quite large and there are other limitations (such as the copy protection of DVDs). Performance typically suffers unacceptably on almost all types of home networks.

Figure 6.1
You can stream video over the Internet, and over your network, using Real Network's RealPlayer

SHARING VIDEO FILES?

Many digital technology experts believe that video will soon be widely shared from one person to another, in much the same way that people now share audio files. Especially as home networks get faster, it's likely that movies and TV shows will be Napsterized—downloaded and traded among users. It's a copyright infringing nightmare for movie companies and TV networks, which are already thinking about ways to counter video file trading. Products like Snapstream (www.snapstream.com), which lets you copy TV programs to your hard drive and share them over a network, are breaking ground in this new territory.

What Type of Network Is Best for Sharing Music and Video?

Choosing the best network for multimedia takes a little more thought than setting up a network for file and Internet sharing. Because networks were not initially designed to carry multimedia, if audio and video playback is important to you, you should consider a network that is specifically designed for this purpose.

Phoneline and powerline products, which are acceptable for audio playback, such as MP3s, are not appropriate for carrying video over your network. Their top speed of 10 mbps results in jerky motion when played from one computer to another.

For all the convenience of 802.11b (Wi-Fi), this wireless technology is not known for its multimedia capabilities. A better choice is to purchase wireless networking hardware that is designed to handle multimedia. These products play music and video more smoothly than some of their wireless counterparts, but the cost is sometimes comparable with other wireless products (see the section on Sharing Music and Video Wirelessly).

The makers of HomeRF wireless networking equipment (see Figure 6.2) argue that their technology is better suited to multimedia than is Wi-Fi (802.11b). The second generation of the HomeRF standard, HomeRF 2.0, is slightly slower than Wi-Fi (10 mbps rather than 11 mbps). However, HomeRF uses a different technology than Wi-Fi, which gives priority to multimedia transmissions, providing them with more bandwidth so that audio and video come across cleanly.

Another benefit of HomeRF is its capability to carry cordless phone calls. However, despite these multimedia and telephony features, HomeRF hasn't quite captured the attention of home networkers, and is much less widely adopted than Wi-Fi. Wi-Fi had its start in business environments, which makes a stronger case for those who want to use wireless networking at home and at work. Also, note that HomeRF and Wi-Fi are incompatible.

A newer version of HomeRF technology, HomeRF 3, will support speeds of 25 mbps and should be handy with music and video on a home network. You can find more about HomeRF at www.homerf.org.

Figure 6.2

The Symphony line of HomeRF wireless networking products from Proxim isn't the fastest networking technology around, but the hardware is specially designed to handle multimedia—here are a USB and PC Card network adapter along with an access point

The newest wireless networking standard, 802.11a is a good choice for both video and audio. Manufacturers claim the technology is five times faster than 802.11b, though the networks do not consistently operate at this speed. Still, 802.11a is currently the best choice for wireless networking that carries multimedia.

It's a little early to tell how 802.11a (also called Wi-Fi5) technology will fare with multimedia. Given its increased speed, the results should impress audio and videophiles. But 802.11b and 802.11a are incompatible, so those who have already started using 802.11b are out of luck. And, at the time of this writing, 802.11a equipment is hard to get, and a good bit more expensive than 802.11b equipment—about $150 per network adapter. You can find an 802.11b network adapter for a bit more than half the price of an 802.11a model.

CONSISTENCY OF SPEED

Many networks, especially wireless networks, do not consistently achieve the top speeds claimed by vendors. In my testing, for example, wireless 802.11b networks, with a top speed of 11 mbps, routinely average less than half that speed. In my experience, although 802.11a networks offer a top speed of 54 mbps, the average speed is actually about twice as fast as 802.11b.

If you prefer to use a wired network, Ethernet can certainly get the job done. Folks who are already using a wired network (for instance, in a home office) appreciate that Ethernet is well suited for multimedia.

Ethernet is fast (10-100mbps) and cheap (about $20 per machine, where 802.11a runs more than $150 per machine).

Drawbacks? You still have to deal with the hassle of running Ethernet cable around the house to connect your computers together. In addition, you can't roam with Ethernet, as you can with wireless, which takes some of the fun out of being able to play your MP3s on your laptop, anywhere in the house. You must stay within cable's reach of your Ethernet hub.

Sharing Music and Video Wirelessly

To share audio and video wirelessly around the house, you can typically take one of several routes:

▶ Purchase network hardware that provides the fastest data transfers, such as 802.11a, because audio and video are bandwidth hungry.

▶ Use a wireless network setup that allows you to connect all your computers together and that is designed to carry multimedia (not all are; see previous section).

▶ Purchase hardware that is specifically designed to let you listen to music stored on your computer on your home stereo.

An example of hardware designed for multimedia is the Panasonic KX-HGW200 Concourse Broadband Networking Gateway and the KX-HGC200 PC Card (see Figures 6.3 and 6.4). The hardware uses enhanced wireless technology, called Sharewave Whitecap, that makes video much more fluid and audio play with fewer dropouts. The catch? These products are not interoperable with wireless 802.11b (Wi-Fi) products. They do, however, offer the ability to connect, through the gateway, to phoneline and Ethernet networks.

Figure 6.3/Figure 6.4
The Panasonic KX-HGW200 Concourse Broadband Networking Gateway is another networking system that is tuned for multimedia; like HomeRF, the hardware is incompatible with 802.11b and 802.11a equipment

Another manufacturer that produces multimedia-friendly networking hardware is Netgear. The company offers a product line that is specifically designed to carry audio and video over a wireless home network. The Netgear WA301 is a wireless network adapter that offers a top speed of 11 mbps and is designed to play Internet video and MP3 audio files.

Yet another choice: X-10 Inc. sells a range of products, most less than $70, that allow you to connect your PC to your stereo or TV. A video product lets you play DVDs on a TV and an audio product lets you play MP3s on a home stereo, both wirelessly. Each comes with a remote.

FOR MORE INFORMATION ON X-10 INC.
X-10, known for products that automate appliances over home electrical wiring, also makes wireless video and audio products. You can find more about X-10 at www.x10.com.

Sharing Video

As network hardware gets faster and new equipment is introduced with enhancements for multimedia, we'll see video become more popular on home networks. For now, however, sharing full-screen video is a bit difficult.

Web Video

Watching video over the network should be straightforward, and, in a way, it is. You can watch small MPEG and QuickTime video files, such as those you might download off the Web. You need to install a movie player on the PC on which you want to watch the movie. *Streaming* video allows you to watch a movie before the entire file has downloaded. Three movie players that are commonly used for watching video that plays or streams over the Web include:

▶ **QuickTime** (Figure 6.5)—www.apple.com/quicktime

▶ **Windows Media Player**—www.microsoft.com/windows/ windowsmedia

▶ **RealPlayer**—www.real.com

Your enjoyment of these movies likely depends more on the speed of your Internet connection than the speed of your network. Any home networking technology should adequately handle playback of small MPEG and QuickTime movies.

Figure 6.5
QuickTime
player—offered
by Apple on its
Web site as a free
download—is
great for viewing
high-quality (if small)
movies on the Web

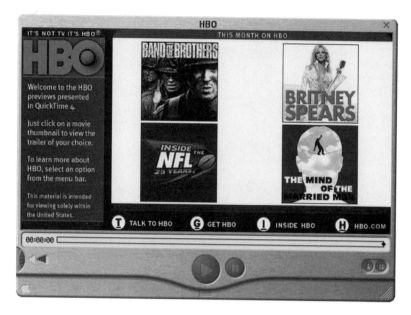

DVD

Unfortunately, the computer and movie industries have yet to embrace the idea of full-screen DVD over a network. There is not yet a simple way of opening a commercial DVD movie over your network.

You can download movie players to watch a movie on your computer's DVD drive—if you have one. For example, you can download WinDVD at www.intervideo.com, as pictured in Figure 6.6. However, the program won't allow you to open a DVD that's not on a local hard drive. It's just not set up to handle the task. The movie industry also puts copy protections on DVDs, which makes the process of playing a DVD from one machine to another on the network even more difficult.

In the future, we expect to see full support of DVD over home networks. For now, however, you're best off watching a movie locally (on the PC where the DVD drive is located) or on a home DVD player connected to your television.

Figure 6.6
WinDVD is a handy
tool for playing DVDs
on your computer;
however, playing
DVDs over a home
network is currently
not an easy task

PC Video or Video Teleconferencing

You can also use built-in (and free) Windows software for video teleconferencing. For instance, you can communicate with others using your Internet connection as a sort of video phone, or you can use video from PC to PC in your house (for example, to keep an eye on things downstairs or to have a video phone intercom in your home).

Windows computers come pre-installed with NetMeeting, a program you can use for audio and video teleconferencing. Windows XP computers use Windows Messenger.

You need a camera installed on your computer. You can purchase a simple Web camera that plugs into your USB port on your computer for less than $70. After your camera is installed, you can start using NetMeeting.

NetMeeting

NetMeeting can be a pain to start because you must click a handful of menus to open it and there's no shortcut directly on the Start menu in Windows. Here's a quick way to open NetMeeting from your PC (see Figure 6.7).

    1.   Click the Start button, and then select Run.

    2.   Type the word "conf".

    3.   Click OK and NetMeeting launches.

Alternatively, you can select Start > Programs (or All Programs in Windows XP) > Accessories > Communications > NetMeeting.

Figure 6.7
Microsoft NetMeeting is bundled free on Windows computers, but it's not always easy to find; the simplest way to start NetMeeting is to use the Run dialog box, from the Start menu in Windows

You can use a PC video camera—connected to your computer, usually through a USB port (or using a video capture card you install)—to display a picture of yourself. If you don't have a camera, you can still connect with other users who do have a camera (see Figure 6.8).

Figure 6.8
Connect a video camera to a PC and you've got an easy-to-use and inexpensive videophone or baby monitor

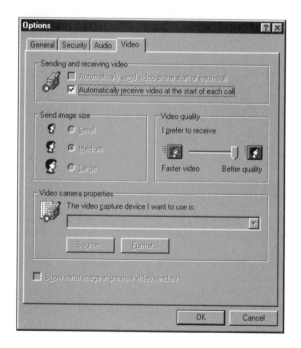

Windows Messenger

Windows Messenger is a handy chat program that supports video, as shown in Figure 6.9. You can download the program from the Microsoft Web site for free. However, only the version for XP supports videoconferencing. Those with operating systems from Windows 98 or earlier will do better to use Microsoft NetMeeting (see the previous section).

If you don't have a video camera, you might find that the chat features of Microsoft Windows Messenger are a helpful addition to your network. Likewise, America Online offers its own free AOL Instant Messenger at www.aol.com.

UPDATING WINDOWS XP MESSENGER

If you want to connect a digital video camera, you might need to first download an update to Windows XP Messenger. You can get the update at:
http://www.microsoft.com/downloads or
http://messenger.jonathankay.com/downloads/q310507.exe

Figure 6.9
Windows
Messenger offers
videoconferencing
features and
comes bundled
in Windows XP

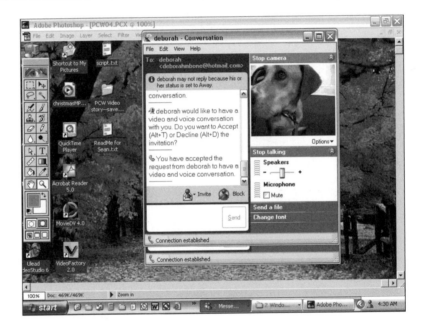

Sharing Music (PC to Stereo)

Sharing music from one PC to another, or from your PC to your stereo, is a great way to have fun and get more use from your network. First, of course, you need some music on your PC. That means putting a CD in a drive that's shared on the network, or better yet, converting your CDs to compressed MP3 files on a PC's hard drive that's available on the network.

The most recent version of Windows Media Player, as shown in Figure 6.10, can do the job. You can download the free program at www.microsoft.com/mediaplayer.

Figure 6.10
Windows Media Player
lets you copy (or burn)
music files to your
hard drive that you
can share over
your network

You can copy a CD audio file to your hard drive using Windows Media Player by per-
forming the following steps.

1. Put an audio CD in your CD drive, then start Windows Media Player (from
the Start menu).

2. Select Copy from CD.

3. Select the songs you want to copy to your hard drive.

4. Click the Copy Music button and wait. The program shows its progress
as it copies each audio track. The files are converted to MP3, by default,
and stored in the My Music folder, under My Documents on your primary
hard drive.

You can also download music files to your hard drive in MP3 format and share them.
MP3 files are a popular format because they are highly compressed (meaning they take up
much less space on your hard drive than a CD audio file). We won't get into the specifics
and legal issues of MP3 files here, but you can certainly find plenty of legal digital music
on the Web (check out www.mp3.com, for starters).

Here are two ways you can enjoy digital music files on your network:

▶ You can copy a file from one computer to another.

▶ You can play the file directly from one computer to another.

First, you need to share the drive where the music is stored.

1. Right-click the drive you want to share.

2. Select Sharing from the shortcut menu that appears.

3. Select the Share this folder option button.

4. Add a password requirement, if you like, and then click OK.

To open the file on your computer, find the file using Network Neighborhood.

1. Open Network Neighborhood and find the computer that contains the music you want to listen to.

2. Open the folder.

3. Double-click the audio file to listen to the music. The program that is associated with this file type opens and starts playing the audio file (see Figure 6.11).

Figure 6.11
To start the music, double-click an audio file on a shared computer

OPENING AUDIO FILES

To quickly associate MP3 files with the program you want to open them, try this trick: Hold the shift key down as you right-click on the type of file you want to open (an MP3 file, or WMA, Windows Media File, for example). When the short-cut menu appears, choose Open With. Select the program that you want to open your audio files. Select the box that says "Always open files of this type with this program." That's it. Now your files will open with the music player you've chosen.

NETWORK NEIGHBORHOOD VS. MY NETWORK PLACES

On Windows 2000, Me, and XP, instead of a Network Neighborhood folder, you'll find a My Network Places folder.

7

Do You Want to Play a Game?

In the 1984 film *War Games*, a computer at the Defense Department asks actor Matthew Broderick if he wants to play a network game. The games we have in mind are slightly less complicated to set up and, thankfully, much less dangerous.

In this chapter, you find out how to connect over your network, and over the Internet, to play multiplayer games. What types of games? Network games come in all sorts of flavors. You can play:

► First-person action games, such as *Doom*

► Role-playing games that borrow heavily from *Dungeons and Dragons*

► Sports games, such as golf or hockey

► Board games, such as Checkers and Chess

► Card games, including Blackjack, Poker, Spades, Hearts, and Bridge

► Word games, vocabulary quizzes, crossword puzzles, and so on

LATENCY AND NETWORK GAMES

With network games, latency is an issue. Latency is the time between the request for information and when it starts to download. Excessive latency causes jerky game play. Over the Internet, latency is to be expected. Playing a graphic-intensive game, such as Quake, works much better over a home network than it does over the Internet.

Playing Network Games

Multiplayer games have been around since the 1970s. Early games, called MUDs (Multi-player Underground Dungeons), were text-based games in which players interacted online. The sort of graphics-heavy games we play today really got their start with the game *Doom*, which was released in 1991. College students, supplied with fast Internet connections paid for by their universities, jumped on the bandwagon and played through the night until it was time to leave for their 8 a.m. classes.

Now, many games offer multiplayer features that allow you to play at home, on your local area network, or over the Internet.

OK, so there are all sorts of games available for network play. But, how do you actually get them and use them? Using your Internet connection, you can save yourself a trip to the software store and download them. Typically, you can get started with a network game in two ways.

▶ **Use your Web browser**. Online games take place within the interface of your Internet browser. You dial up an address, such as the gaming sites from Yahoo or the Microsoft Network (MSN). Browser-based games include card games, such as Spades or Poker, and board games like Checkers, Chess, and Backgammon (see Figure 7.1).

▶ **Download a game (or purchase a CD-ROM)**. After you purchase the game in a store or download it, you can install and play the game over a local area network (LAN) or the Internet. Typically, this type of game must be installed to your hard drive. The game is played in a custom-programmed interface (not your Internet browser).

Online, browser-based games load small applications into the browser each time you play. You download the game to your hard drive, but the games do not *install* on your hard drive in the way most of your programs do. They operate in a protected space, and you need to wait for them to download each time you want to play. That said, you might need to download a small program, such as Macromedia's Shockwave, and install it on your hard drive, to allow the games to play.

More complicated, hard-drive hungry, and expensive network games require that you purchase them at a store, or download them over the Internet, and install them on your home machine. Thankfully, games, such as id Software's Quake (www.idsoftware.com), often provide a shareware version for download that lets you try the game before you buy it. These trialware games sometimes include multiplayer capability, allowing you to play over your network.

Sophisticated 3D games, such as Quake (shown in Figure 7.2), are highly customizable. You can download all sorts of files to update the look and play of the game, and users with programming skills can even create their own scenes.

Figure 7.1
The MSN Gaming Zone site offers a wide range of browser-based games

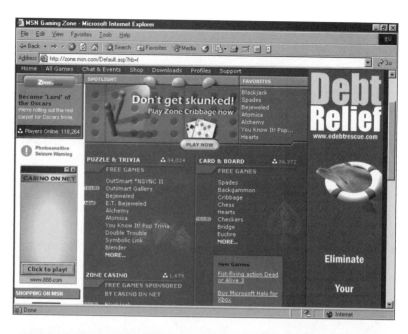

Figure 7.2
Quake is one of the more popular network-based games; players from all over the world can compete against each other in this graphic and testosterone-heavy game

DO YOU KNOW YOUR IP ADDRESS?

Sometimes, network games that you play over your LAN require you to know your IP address to start playing. Your IP address is a unique number that identifies your computer on your network or on the Internet. Most often, you use one IP address that identifies you on the Internet. Your software or hardware router creates sub-addresses, which are used on your network but not on the Internet. You can find your IP address using a Windows program called winipcfg. Select Start > Run, type winipcfg in the text box, and then click Enter. A dialog box appears that displays your IP address.

Hardware Considerations for Gamers

Network gaming adds a competitive element, letting you go head-to-head with your opponents, rather than simply playing against a computer. Network games tend to be more interesting and faster-paced than single-player games. Although games you play in your Web browser aren't terribly demanding on your computer, multiplayer computer games you install on your hard drive push your system to its limits.

Computer Hardware

Graphically-complex network games are about the most processor-intensive task you'll ask your computer to take on. These games are incredibly demanding, and the latest games require serious processing power, high-end video cards, and gobs of memory. It's ironic that fun comes at such a cost—you'll find that "gamer" systems are the most costly available. It's an expensive hobby.

Many of the graphic-intensive multiplayer games use 3D imaging. Your computer needs to redraw complex images on-screen in a split second. Your computer requires a 3D card to handle some of the work of drawing the backgrounds, character movement, and special effects.

Plus, these games eat hundreds of megabytes of your hard drive. In addition, complex sound effects and sophisticated soundtracks are the mark of a good multiplayer game, and you'll want a reasonable sound system to get the most out of the experience.

Almost any Pentium laptop provides the capability to play online games in your Internet browser. Complex 3D games are more demanding. You can get away with an older processor, but you need a good 3D graphics card, ideally with at least 32 MB of RAM, which helps store data in memory and results in faster game play. You can expect to pay between $150 and $300 for a good graphics card.

Networking Hardware

In a local area network (LAN), you can play your friends and family in very graphic-intensive games, such as Unreal Tournament, a 3D shoot-'em-up game, with detailed environments (sometimes called "maps") and lifelike characters. These types of games benefit from the fastest networking hardware you can buy. Ethernet and fast wireless hardware, such as 802.11a (see Figure 7.3), are better suited for these types of games than are phoneline or older wireless technologies, such as 802.11b.

If you plan to play online 3D games, consider a broadband modem rather than a 56 kbps analog modem. Slower modems lead to jerky game play. In these life-and-death situations, you want all the speed you can get!

Figure 7.3
An 802.11a network offers a maximum speed of 54 mbps, well-suited for network gaming

How Do Home Network Games Work?

So, how does a network game work? Typically, whether the game is played on a LAN or the Internet, one computer is set up to act as the server or host. After the host is running and ready to accept connections, the other players log on to the server. The server checks to make sure each player has the correct version of the game and the associated files, and then allows the player to join the game.

Multiplayer games use many of the terms that you hear used for networking. The following sections define these terms.

Host/Server

The host or server is the computer everyone logs onto to play a multiplayer game. Most multiplayer games come with a server feature that lets you "host" other players on your computer to play at the same time. If your computer is the host, the computers that log on to your server are the "clients." As each player moves his character or takes some other action, such as firing a weapon, the server sends this information to all the clients.

Client

A client is the computer that connects to a server to play a multiplayer game. A client can log on to a server on a local area network or through the Internet. The amount of time it takes for a command to be sent by your client to a server is called the ping time. You want a server with the shortest ping time available.

Internet games you play using your browser, such as those at Yahoo and MSN, are often played using a small program called a Java applet. Java is a handy computer language, because it allows software programmers to write the program once for many platforms, such as PCs, Macs, and even UNIX machines.

Other online games use a browser add-on, called a plug-in, such as Macromedia's Shockwave or Flash plug-ins. These are the most common types of browser-based online games, although others are created in standard computer languages, such as C and Visual Basic.

Getting Started With Multiplayer Games

You can hop on the Internet at any time and find willing participants for an online game. Although many multiplayer games are capable of playing over a LAN, the Internet offers an easy way to find online gamers whenever you're ready to play.

A number of game services are available that let you find other players for all types of games, and offer downloads that can make the games operate optimally. We look at these in the last section of this chapter.

NETWORK GAMING TIP

Want to pick up a few tips and tricks about network gaming? Here's a helpful site that can point you in the right direction: http://compnetworking.about.com.

Here's how to get started with a multiplayer game on the Net.

1. Log on to your site of choice, for instance MSN (zone.msn.com) or Yahoo (games.yahoo.com). You don't need to sign up for an account to play some of the games at MSN, but you do need to register for a free account to play any of the games at Yahoo. (See Figure 7.4.)

2. Enter your username and password.

3. Select the game you want to play.

Keep in mind that the type of game you choose might dictate the sort of social environment you can expect to encounter when gaming online. A 3D action game tends to throw you to the wolves, virtually speaking. These folks tend to spend quite a bit of time perfecting their skills. You might find yourself quickly outmaneuvered by trash-talking twelve-year-olds. Did I mention that many multiplayer games have a chat feature? The level of discourse in a 3D shooter is pretty much what you might expect. If you're new to online gaming, give yourself some time to check out how folks deal with each other. In contrast, online board, word, and card games tend to be quite civilized and much easier to jump into for first-timers.

Figure 7.4
Ready to meet some
Yahooligans? Sign in at
Yahoo Games

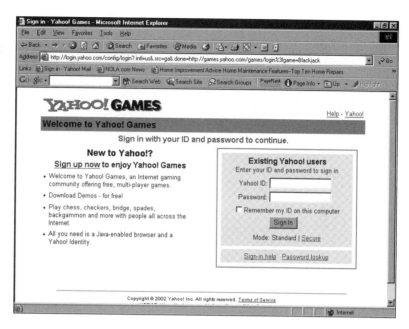

CHAPTER 7

Let Your Computer Host a Game

Network games are often capable of hosting other players on your computer. Hosting a game is simple. In fact, most network games handle most of the work for you. You'll likely need your IP address (see the previous tip about finding your IP address with winipcfg).

1. Start your game, and enter the multiplayer mode (games vary slightly, but most have an Options screen).

2. Choose the command to start your network server.

3. Invite other players to join your network server. (They follow these steps, but instead of choosing the start server command, they choose the join server command.)

You might need to provide players with your IP address. If you're playing on the Internet, you need the IP address that your ISP provides you. Some games search for the server on your network and log the players on automatically.

Graphic-intensive 3D games require a lot of processing power. Interestingly, these games are programmed so that only a small amount of data is sent over the network, so, although they may keep your processor churning away, the action of the game isn't slowed down by the network connection.

To get a quick idea of how 3D multiplayer games work, here's how to play Quake over a local network or over the Internet.

1. Start the game and, from the opening screen, enter multiplayer mode (see Figure 7.5).

2. Click to join a server, which searches the network for an available server.

3. If you're playing on a LAN, a list of the available servers appears. Select the one you want to join and click Enter.

4. If you want to play using a server on the Internet, enter the IP address of the server and click Enter.

5. Start playing, and watch your back!

Figure 7.5
You can log on to a Quake server on your network using the multiplayer mode of the game

FINDING MORE INFORMATION ABOUT QUAKE

You can find available Quake servers on the Internet, as well as more information about multiplayer Quake, at www.stomped.com.

Where to Find Online Games

Online games, especially those that are played within the Web browser, are a very popular and easy way to get started playing games over your network. Keep in mind that although you need an Internet connection to play, all your computers can connect simultaneously after your computers are networked, allowing everybody in your family to play over the Net at once.

Yahoo is probably the most popular place to find other gamers (see Figures 7.6 and 7.7). You'll see all sorts of multiplayer games, the usual card and board game fare, and even games where you can find a partner—MahJong for instance—and take on other Yahoo players. The Yahoo Games site also has single-player games if you're not feeling competitive.

If you've never played an online game, you might have some concerns—we will address these in the following sections.

Cost

The majority of online, browser-based games are free, and the sites support the cost of game play through advertising. In some cases, you can download, and pay for, a version of the game so you won't have to load it into your browser each time you play.

Security

Java games in particular are designed to work inside a safe area of your computer where they can't affect other files on your hard drive. A Java applet from a trusted Web site, such as Yahoo, isn't likely to cause any damage to your system, so play worry free. Furthermore, online games are controlled by a central server. Players don't have access to your computer when you play an online game.

Online Games and Kids

The online games mentioned here are primarily PC versions of board and card games. Parents should give some thought to which online games they allow kids to play, but it's not hard to find age-appropriate games online. Some of the 3D multiplayer games, in contrast to online, browser-based games, tend to push the limits of both your computer and your sense of appropriateness. You can find game ratings online, which might help as you decide what kinds of games are right for your kids: Check out the Entertainment Software Ratings Board for searchable game listings at www.esrb.org.

Figure 7.6
You can find other gamers on Yahoo—each game listing displays the number of people currently playing at one time

Figure 7.7
Select a game and you are shown various "rooms" from which you can pick; the games offer instant messaging so that you can chat with other players in the room you choose—who needs Vegas?

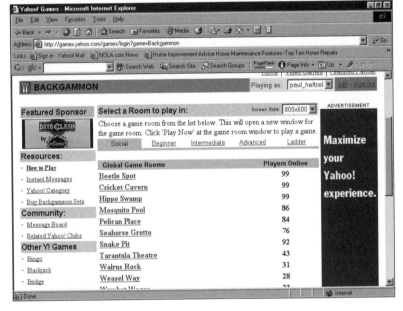

ENGLISH GAMING

Got a family member who's always quoting Monty Python? A boss who follows English football? Point the Anglophile in your life to the BBC's gaming site: http://www.bbc.co.uk/games.

Shockwave.com (www.shockwave.com)

Shockwave is a program from software-maker Macromedia that you install on your computer so that you can view multimedia. Shockwave.com offers some of the best gaming around, and at file sizes that won't make you suffer through interminable downloads (see an example in Figure 7.8). My personal favorites are the 80s arcade games: www.shockwave.com/sw/games/arcade/classics. You can play single-player games, or get everybody on your network to log on and play at the same time.

Figure 7.8
The Shockwave site has some of the best games online

EA.com (Electronic Arts)

This site has some of the most sophisticated online gaming available. On the far end of the spectrum from the low-fi look of Yahoo, EA.com offers driving games, sports games, and other 3D games you can play with others or by yourself (see Figure 7.9). Downloads typically take longer than other sites, but you're rewarded with elegant graphics.

Figure 7.9
EA.com offers advanced online games, rivaling those you purchase and install on your hard drive

Yahoo (games.yahoo.com)

As on just about everything else related to the Internet, Yahoo has put its imprint on Internet gaming. Like other Yahoo offerings, the site trades fancy graphics for speed and reliability. If you enjoy board and card games, Yahoo is the place to be (see Figure 7.10).

Figure 7.10
Yahoo hosts thousands of game players at a time

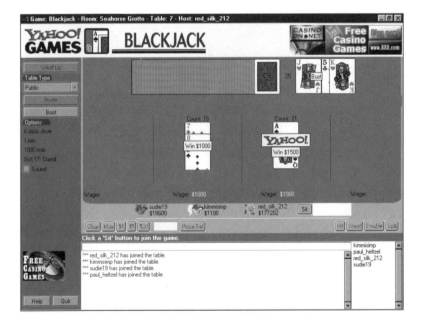

MSN Gaming Zone (www.zone.com)

The Zone, like Yahoo, provides broad offerings. Unlike Yahoo, MSN hosts action and adventure games as well as Sims (simulators), such as Fighter Ace, a pay for play game (see Figure 7.11).

Figure 7.11
MSN offers online simulators, such as Fighter Ace

Coffee Break Arcade (www.coffeebreakarcade.com)

Coffee Break Arcade, as shown in Figure 7.12, lists games that are hosted on various Web sites. The site provides game descriptions, instructions on how to play, and a direct link that starts the games.

Figure 7.12
Checking out game
listings at Coffee
Break Arcade

Uproar (www.uproar.com)

Uproar hosts a large collection of familiar TV game shows, including Family Feud and
Name That Tune (see Figure 7.13).

Figure 7.13
Uproar offers online
game shows

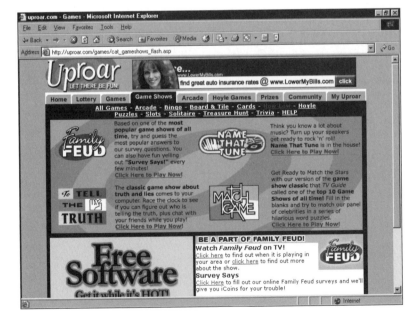

Flipside (www.flipside.com)

The Flipside site, brought to you by the same folks that produce Uproar, offers Vegas-style games (with no wagering), and they offer cash prizes for lottery games and a treasure hunt. (See Figure 7.14.)

Figure 7.14
Flipside offers no-wager casino games as well as board games and a lottery

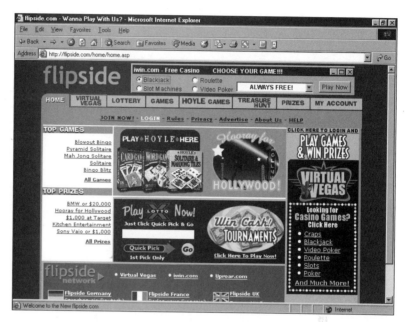

NETWORK GAME REVIEWS AND DOWNLOADS

You can find more about network games—as well as reviews and downloads—at the GamePen (gamepen.ugo.com) and GameSpy (www.gamespy.com) sites.

8

Sharing the Internet

In many homes, Internet access is much coveted, especially if there is only one available phone line. Whether you use an analog or broadband modem, you can use your network to provide Internet access to all the computers in your house.

Internet sharing might sound complicated, but the fine people at Microsoft have actually made the job straightforward. The catch is that different versions of Windows need to be set up slightly differently. Windows 95 and 98 have a different setup process than Windows Me, 2000, and XP. These more recent Windows operating systems (Me through XP) include network setup wizards, which automates much of the process.

Another useful Windows feature is called Internet Connection Sharing (ICS). In particular, if you do not have a hardware device called a router, you'll want to get to know ICS. Routers, as mentioned previously, help your network connect to the Internet. ICS lets one of the computers on your network share its Internet connection with all the other computers on your LAN.

Setting up Internet access is probably the trickiest home networking job you'll take on. It can take half an hour to connect a few computers, or it can take a long, painful weekend. Before you get started, make sure you are ready with this quick checklist. It's often the simple things that hold you up.

▶ Have the information your Internet Service Provider sent you regarding connecting to the Internet. This is important, as installation procedures vary widely.

▶ Make sure all your network adapters are connected and that they are connected to each other, or to your hub.

▶ Check to ensure that your DSL, cable, or analog 56 kbps modem is plugged in and able to connect to the Internet. Don't try to set up both your new DSL modem, for example, and your network all at the same time—you'll be asking for trouble. After you know one of your computers can connect to the Net, then work on sharing access.

▶ Especially with Windows 95/98, have your operating system disk handy. You might be prompted to insert it when setting up your network adapter to connect over the network.

Sharing a Connection

Sharing a connection means sharing a modem. You can share different kinds of modems on your LAN.

▶ **Analog**. Most computers today come with 56 kbps analog modems. An analog modem converts digital signals from your computer to analog signals that can be carried over a phone line.

▶ **DSL**. DSL (Digital Subscriber Line) uses regular phone lines to provide high-speed Internet access to your home.

▶ **Cable Modem**. Cable modems use the same cable line that you use to plug in a TV. Cable modems are the most popular means of getting broadband Internet access to a home.

Sharing an Analog Modem

Most home Internet-sharing networks use a *broadband* connection, which offers speedy surfing to multiple PCs sharing the same DSL or cable modem. As each computer requests data, the maximum throughput of all the other connections is reduced. Bottom line: You want as much speed as possible.

That said, there's no reason why you can't share the 56 kbps modem that's in your desktop or laptop. The benefit? Everybody gets online, even if the speed won't burn any barns. If you can't get or don't want broadband Internet access, set up your dial-up modem for sharing.

Recently, I shared an analog modem when I moved into a new apartment and my DSL modem had not yet arrived. I shared the dial-up connection on my desktop PC with two laptops, wirelessly, using an 802.11b (Wi-Fi) wireless network. Because, in my home, most often, only one person at a time clicks a link or sends an e-mail, the speed is completely adequate. I've tested lots of networking hardware this way, using the Internet Connection Sharing (ICS) feature of Windows XP. ICS works quite well with my analog modem in my home office.

ICS is useful because most routers are not set up to share an analog modem connection. However, the Apple AirPort is a notable exception (see Figure 8.1).

Figure 8.1
The Apple AirPort is a
wireless access point
and router that lets you
share one Internet
connection with
multiple computers,
and it also has a built-
in modem, which you
can share among all
the computers on a
Macintosh network;
the AirPort includes
a firewall and support
for America Online
users (image courtesy
of Apple)

Sharing DSL and Cable Connections

If you have broadband Internet access, you know how much more useful it makes the Internet. The ability to watch short videos, download music, and generally get around the Web at high speeds makes your Internet life much more fun. Networking your Internet access adds another level of enjoyment and usefulness to your fast connection. Now, everybody can get online whenever they want and each computer still accesses the Internet much faster than with a 56 kbps analog modem.

Sharing a broadband connection over a wireless connection is particularly useful. You can surf anywhere in your house, and you'll be able to say goodbye to being tethered to your cable or phone jack.

Wireless networking hardware is focused on sharing broadband connections. The equipment you need for wireless Internet sharing—an access point and router—is widely available. In addition, prices are dropping almost daily. It's a great time to go wireless.

If your house isn't an ideal setup for wireless Internet sharing, you should consider wired options, or potentially, a hybrid network. Hybrid networks let you combine different technologies—for example, 802.11b wireless network hardware mixed with Ethernet hardware—and get the roaming ability of wireless hardware with the speed and reliability of wired hardware.

New hardware that uses your existing house wiring is making hybrid networks an attractive option. If your house is very large, you might find wireless equipment won't cover the distances you need. (Wireless equipment tends to have a range of about 150 feet indoors.) Obstructions, such as walls, brick, concrete, and steel, can quickly reduce the effectiveness of wireless hardware.

Phoneline and powerline hardware is now available, as are routers that use these technologies. Phoneline tends to be the budget choice, with adapters costing less than $50 (see Figure 8.2). A phoneline router costs you about $150-300. Powerline equipment runs about $150 per adapter, and routers cost less than $200.

Figure 8.2
Phoneline network hardware, such as this adapter from Netgear, lets you share Internet access (and files) in your home using your existing house wiring

How a Router Can Help

You can use a router to connect your LAN to the Internet. A router can make your network setup easier in a couple of ways.

▶ A router helps you connect your broadband modem to your network. You don't need to keep one computer on all the time to share your Internet connection. A router handles this job for you.

▶ A router handles the IP addressing for your network, so that each computer can access the Internet.

In a wired network, you install a router by plugging it into your hub or connecting it into the Ethernet port of your broadband modem. You can connect a wired router to a wireless access point, though it's typically easier to use an access point with a built-in router.

After you plug in the router, you should connect to your Internet Service Provider. Sometimes, you need to make changes to the router by adding information provided to you from your ISP. You access the router, after it's connected to your network, through a browser on one of your computers (see Figure 8.3). You type in the IP address of the router (often 192.168.0.1) and are then prompted for a password. (Some routers require you to use a text-based Windows program called Telnet to make changes. Look for a router that offers browser-based configuration, which is much easier to use.)

You need some basic information from your ISP, including your IP address, if you are provided with one. Remember, an IP address is a number that uniquely identifies your computer on your network or on the Internet.

If your provider gives you one address that is always the same, then you have a *static* IP address. Some providers issue you a new IP address at set times, so that they can spread fewer addresses around to more customers. In this case, your IP address is called a *dynamic* address, because it changes at your ISP's discretion.

If your provider uses dynamic addressing (many do), the default settings for your router might do the trick. When this is the case, you might be ready to go as soon as your router is plugged in—no changes necessary. Follow the instructions that came with your hardware and the setup instructions that came from your ISP. If you are unable to connect after you have entered the configuration information from your ISP using your router's configuration tools, it's time to call your ISP's tech support.

Figure 8.3
Input the information provided by your ISP and you are ready to share Internet access with the other PCs on your network

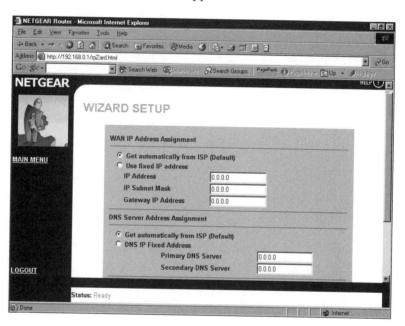

Many routers offer DHCP (Dynamic Host Configuration Protocol), a way to automatically distribute IP addresses to each computer on your network. DHCP saves you from having to enter your IP address manually on each computer. You enable Windows computers to use DHCP in the TCP settings associated with your network card. (See "Set up other computers to obtain IP addresses automatically" later in this chapter.)

NETWORK ADDRESS TRANSLATION
Routers use a feature called NAT (Network Address Translation), which allows you to share one IP address, provided by your ISP, among all the computers on your network.

Connecting with Windows

Windows PCs are actually pretty simple to set up for Internet access. You should have in hand any information from your Internet Service Provider (ISP) before you attempt to get multiple computers on your LAN surfing the Internet. In some cases, you need specific information from your ISP. In other cases, the default settings in Windows work just fine.

We'll discuss two ways to access the Internet using Windows.

▶ Configure a PC to share Internet access. One PC with a connection that's always available is best. You can also set up ICS to dial up your ISP each time a computer on the network tries to connect to the Internet.

▶ Set up your PCs to share access using a router.

Using a router is the preferred way to share Internet access. You won't need a computer dedicated to Internet access. Routers are relatively inexpensive—less than $100. A router allows all your computers to share one IP address, and most handle the assignment of IP addresses to your computers automatically. More on that later.

The Basic Setup

First things first. We need to check and make sure you have a network card installed and that TCP/IP is associated with your network card. Remember earlier in the book, we mentioned that TCP/IP is the language (or protocol) of the Internet. All computers connecting to the Internet, whether they're Macs, PCs, Linux, or any other computer, are communicating via TCP/IP. Associating the protocol with your network card is sometimes called *binding* the protocol. If your network card is installed and you know the TCP/IP protocol is installed, you can skip this section and move on to the next section.

If you have your Windows operating system disk, the one that came with your computer, have it ready. Depending on the version of Windows you are using, and whether you already have TCP/IP installed, you might not need the OS disk. Grab it just in case.

For Windows 95/98, do this:

1. Select Start > Settings > Control Panel. Double-click the Network icon. You can also right-click the Network Neighborhood icon on your desktop to open Network properties. This is where the magic happens. You'll use the Network properties dialog box many times as you set up your network. After your network is active, you'll be pretty well set and won't need to mess with these settings again unless you run into a problem (see Chapter 11, "Troubleshooting").

2. In the area labeled "The following network components are installed," look for your network card. You might need to scroll. If you don't see it, and you know it's installed, you might need to reinstall the drivers. Check the instructions that came with your network card for proper installation instructions. Don't know what kind of network card you have? That's OK.

For Windows 98, right-click the My Computer icon on the desktop, then choose Properties. Click the Device Manager tab. Click the plus sign (+) next to "Network adapters." You should see the name of the card there. If you have Windows XP, open the Device manager. To do this, select Start, then right-click My Computer and choose Properties. Click the Hardware tab, and click the Device Manager button. Click the plus sign next to "Network adapters." You should see the name of your network card there.

3. Scroll down the list under "The following network components are installed."

4. You should see TCP/IP -> next to the name of your network card (see Figure 8.4).

Figure 8.4
Select your network adapter card so you can make changes to the TCP/IP settings

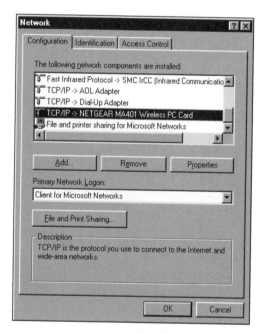

If you see your network card and it is associated with TCP/IP, all is well. If you see your card, but you *don't* see TCP/IP associated with your network card, follow these steps:

1. Insert your operating system CD-ROM into your CD drive.

2. Choose Start > Settings > Control Panel.

3. Double-click the Network Control Panel icon.

4. Click the Add button.

5. Select Protocol and click the Add button.

6. Select Microsoft, then choose TCP/IP.

7. Click OK twice to close the open dialog boxes. You might be prompted for your Windows OS disk. Click OK. You are prompted to restart your computer. Click OK to reboot.

Windows 2000 and XP have the TCP/IP protocol installed by default. If your network card is installed, you should have TCP/IP software already installed on computers running these network-savvy operating systems.

ICS

If you have a dial-up modem rather than broadband (cable or DSL Internet access), you can use ICS for sharing the connection. (See Table 8.1.) If you want to use ICS for connecting to a broadband connection, you need two network adapters (most likely Ethernet) for your computer. One network adapter connects to the broadband modem. The other adapter connects to another computer, hub, or access point.

Table 8.1 Choosing a router or ICS	
If you have:	**Use:**
A broadband modem	An Ethernet router (less than $100) or wireless router and access point (about $150).
Dial-up connection	Windows's free software, Internet Connection Sharing (ICS).

Connecting with Windows 98 Second Edition

Here, we walk through Internet access setup using Windows 98 Second Edition or later. In this example, we assume you are using either a router that provides DHCP or Windows Internet Connection Sharing. You need to choose one or the other to share Internet access between all the computers on your LAN.

First, you set the IP address for your computer by associating the address with your network card. If you are using a router that offers DHCP, you enable DHCP. If your router does not offer this feature, you need to set your IP address manually (see the final section of this chapter).

Install Internet Connection Sharing

First, you need to install Internet Connection Sharing on your computer.

1. Choose Start > Settings > Control Panel.

2. Double-click Add/Remove Programs.

3. Click the Windows Setup tab.

4. Double-click Internet Tools, as shown in Figure 8.5.

5. Choose Internet Connection Sharing (see Figure 8.6) and click OK.

Figure 8.5
Select Internet Tools
so that you can add
Internet Connection
Sharing to Windows 98
Second Edition or later

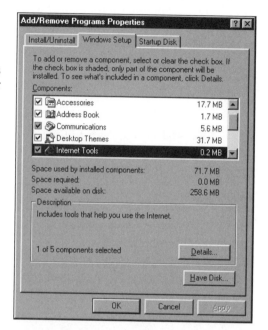

Figure 8.6
Select Internet
Connection Sharing

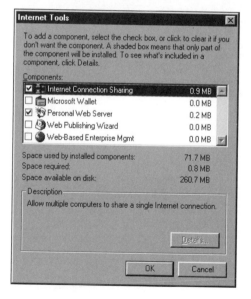

Enable ICS

Next, you need to get ICS up and running so that you can share an Internet connection on your LAN, if you don't use a router.

1. Choose Internet Options from the Control Panel and click the Connections tab.

2. From the LAN Settings area, click the Sharing button (see Figure 8.7).

3. Select your Internet connection.

4. Choose the network adapter you use to connect to your LAN and then click OK (see Figure 8.8).

Figure 8.7
Sharing your
LAN connection

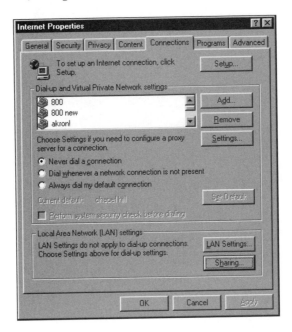

Figure 8.8
Choosing your
network adapter

The Internet Connection Wizard can handle this job for you. From the Control Panel
(select Start > Settings > Control Panel), open Internet Options. Choose the Connections
tab. Click Internet Sharing Settings.

Set up Other Computers to Obtain IP Addresses Automatically

Setting up your computers to obtain their IP addresses automatically is simple and is often
required by your ISP. Whether you use a router or ICS to connect to the Internet, it's good
to know how to set your computers to obtain an IP address automatically, using DHCP.

1. From the Control Panel, choose Network.
2. Choose the TCP/IP network adapter from the list. (See Figure 8.9.)
3. Click Properties.
4. Select Obtain an IP address automatically.
5. If you need to set the IP address manually, your ISP tells you to do so. (You
    won't need to enter in your IP addresses manually if you are using ICS or a
    router that has DHCP.) To set your address manually, click Specify an IP
    address. Enter the address and click OK twice to close the open dialog boxes.

Figure 8.9
Choosing your TCP/IP
network adapter

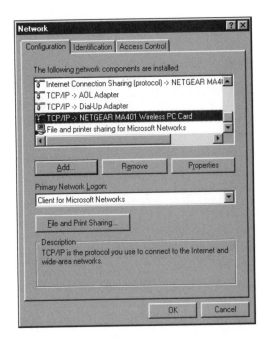

 SETTING IP ADDRESSES
Most often, you won't need to set your own IP addresses. ICS or your router
takes care of this job for you. If your router does not support DHCP, for example,
you use a private IP address where the format is 169.168.0.2 to 192.168.0.253.
Networks that do not connect to the Internet use network addresses in the format
192.254.x.x.

Connecting with Windows XP

On Windows XP computers, the Network Setup Wizard is already installed. This tool can
help you connect all your computers to each other and start sharing the Internet in just a
few minutes. If you run into trouble, the problem might be specific to your hardware or
ISP. If you can't get connected after following these steps and the instructions that came
with your equipment, you need to call tech support.

Enable ICS Using the Network Setup Wizard

1. Start the Network Setup Wizard. To do this, click Start > Control Panel >
   Network Connections. Under Common Tasks, choose Network Setup Wizard.

2. Make sure your Internet connection is active.

3. Click Next several times to advance to the Select a connection
   method screen.

4. Select "This computer connects directly to the Internet." (See Figure 8.10.)

5. Continue clicking Next until the wizard completes, then click the Finish button.

Figure 8.10
Tell Windows XP that
this is the computer
that will share its
Internet connection
on your network

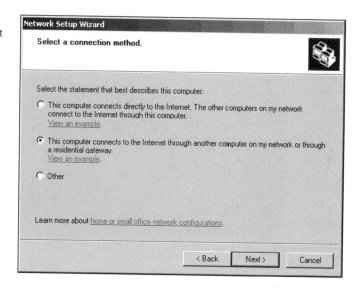

Run Network Setup Wizard on Other Computers

On Windows computers (Windows 98 and later), you can run the Network Setup Wizard so that your computers will connect to your main computer to access the Internet.

1. Insert your Windows XP disk in the drive of the computer you want to access ICS.

2. From the Startup screen, choose Perform additional tasks.

3. Choose Set up a home or small office network (see Figure 8.11).

4. Follow the wizard's instructions, and then reboot.

Figure 8.11
Select the Set up a
home or small office
network option

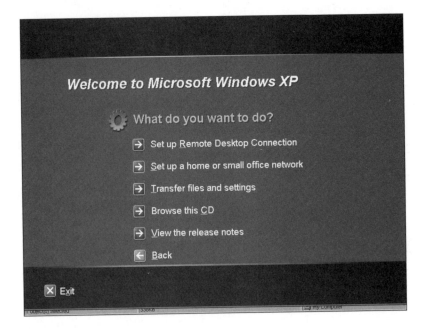

If your ISP tells you to, you can also manually change your network adapter's settings.

1. From the Control Panel, open Network Connections.

2. Right-click the Network connection you want to change and select Properties.

3. Select the General tab (if it isn't already selected), click Internet Protocol TCP/IP, and then choose Properties.

4. Make the changes your ISP recommends.

9

Remote Access

What good is a network when you're on the road? If you leave a file at home or need to quickly use a program that you don't have installed on your laptop while you travel, remote access to your network can be a huge help.

Creating a fast and rewarding telecommuting setup is remarkably simple. You might already have the software needed to get started with remote access. Most Windows computers come with a program called Microsoft NetMeeting installed, which allows you to share programs remotely. Other, more feature-filled (and more expensive) remote access programs let you call up your home or work computer and control the computer over the Internet—just as if you were sitting in front of the computer you want to use. In this chapter, you'll learn all about how to access files at home from the office, or access office files from home.

Why Connect Remotely?

If you take work home, you know that leaving a file behind can be a show stopper. There's no way to e-mail it to yourself after you're home, and unless you have remote access software, you're pretty much stuck. Remote access gives you a sense of security, so you don't have to burn every file you need to a CD or copy them to a floppy each time you leave home or work.

You can use free programs, often bundled in Windows operating systems, or you can purchase third-party software that typically offers more features. In this chapter, we discuss Symantec pcAnywhere and LapLink (see Figure 9.1), two of the most popular third-party software packages for remote access. Refer to Table 9.1 to compare some of the various remote access software packages.

CHAPTER 9

Figure 9.1
LapLink lets you access files on one computer from another, over the Internet or through a direct modem connection; you can use Laplink to control a remote computer, just as if you were sitting in front of it

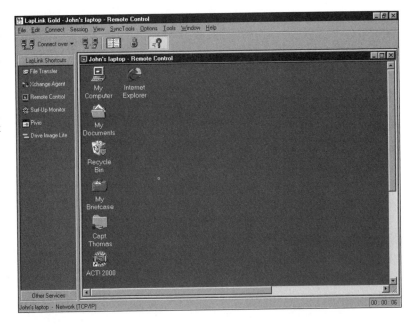

Table 9.1 Remote Access Software Features Comparison		
Program	**Pro/Con**	**Cost**
NetMeeting	Free/Limited features	Free
LapLink	Plenty of features for telecommuters and travelers/Costly	$180
Symantec pcAnywhere	Full-featured/Costly	$180

Connecting to Your Home Network by Modem

You might be surprised to know that Windows offers remote access, through a program called Dial-Up Server that has been bundled with the operating system since Windows 95 (in the Windows 95 Plus add-on package). The primary hang-up is that it's unable to connect over the Internet. The computer you want to access needs a modem, connected to a phone line, waiting for the call.

Make a Direct Modem Connection

Here's how to make a direct modem connection in Windows 98. This setup allows you to share files and printers on your computer at home when you're out on the road. You should have your Windows 98 disk handy. You need to copy the Dial-Up Server program from the Windows 98 disk. Ready to become a server? Let's get started.

Setting up Your Home Computer

You need to set up both your home computer and the remote computer. On your home computer, perform the following steps.

1. First, install the Dial-Up Server. Open the Control Panel (Start > Settings > Control Panel) and double-click Add/Remove Programs. Select the Windows Setup tab, as shown in Figure 9.2.

2. Double-click Communications and then select Dial-Up Server. Click OK twice to accept your changes and close open dialog boxes. You are prompted to insert your Windows 98 disk.

3. Now, you need to set up your computer to accept incoming calls. From My Computer, double-click the Dial-Up Networking folder.

4. From that folder, choose the Connections menu, and choose Dial-Up Server (as shown in Figure 9.3).

5. Select Allow caller access, click the Password button, enter a new password (you don't need to enter an old password), confirm that password, and then click OK. See Figure 9.4.

6. Set up file and printer sharing and share a file. (See Chapter 5, "Sharing Data and Equipment" for details on setting up file and printer sharing.)

Figure 9.2
To get started installing the Dial-Up Server, choose the Windows Setup tab

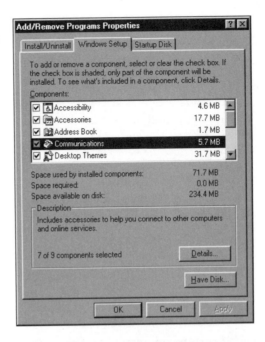

Figure 9.3
Select the Dial-Up Server to start installation of the applet from your Windows 98 disk

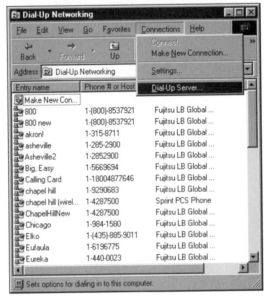

Figure 9.4
Create a password for
your connection

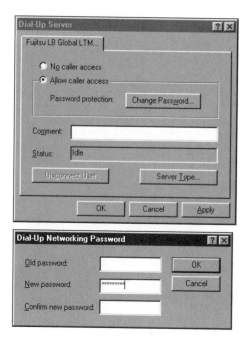

Setting Up Your Remote Computer

After you install and set up Dial-Up Server on the machine to which you want to connect, you need to configure the computer that dials into your home computer. It's as easy
as setting up the dial-up networking connection to your ISP. On your remote computer,
perform the following steps.

1. Under My Computer, open Dial-Up Networking.
2. Double-click Make New Connection (see Figure 9.5).
3. Give your connection a name you'll remember.
4. Enter the phone number of the line to which your home computer is
   connected.
5. From the Dial-Up Networking folder, double-click your new connection to
   open it. Enter the password you created in the previous set of steps (see
   Figure 9.6).
6. Click the Connect button to dial up your computer.

CHAPTER 9

Figure 9.5
Double-click the Make
New Connection icon

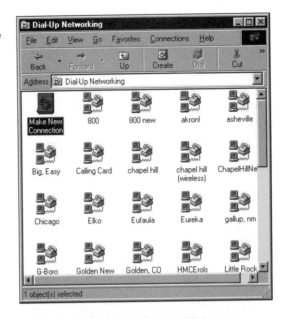

Figure 9.6
Enter the password you
created in the previous
set of steps, and your
home phone number
(or the number of the
phone line your
modem is connected
to, if different)

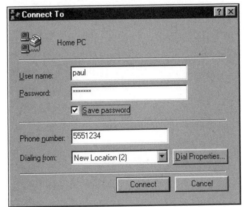

After you connect, you can access your files and printers, just as if you were at home,
connected to your network.

1. Double-click Network Neighborhood to see what resources are available on
    the network.

2. Open a shared folder (see Figure 9.7).

3. You can view shared resources over your dial-up connection and copy
    files and folders from your remote computer to your home computer.

Figure 9.7
You can connect by
modem to your
computer and access
your home network

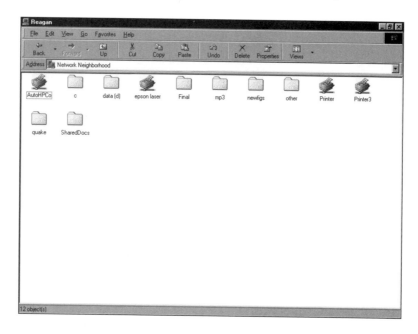

Make an Internet Connection

As we discussed in the last section, Dial-Up Server is a free utility included in newer versions of Windows. The applet is handy if you have a modem connected to the home PC you want to access. But what if you want to connect over the Internet, for instance from work over a T-1 line? And, at home, your PC might not be connected to a phone line. Maybe it's connected to a fast cable or DSL modem connection.

Here, we show you how to connect to a remote computer, over any Internet connection, using the popular LapLink Gold software. The directions are specific to LapLink, but most programs of this type work in a similar way.

Follow these steps to share the desktop of a remote computer running LapLink. You need to have LapLink installed and running on both computers.

1. To give your home PC a name that you'll use when connecting from the road, choose Options > Computer Name.
2. Enter a name you'll remember in the Computer Name dialog box, as shown in Figure 9.8. (For example, you might use an e-mail address or something else that you can easily remember.)
3. Click OK.

Figure 9.8
Give your home PC a
name you'll use to
connect to it

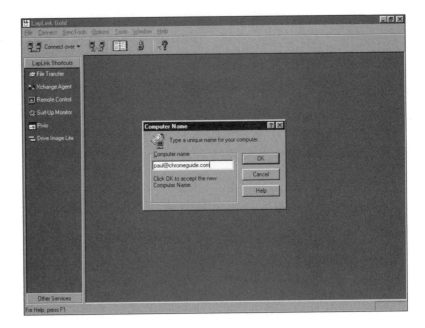

Now, let's connect to the host computer (the one for which you just set up a name).

1. Click Connect over, and then select Internet, as shown in Figure 9.9.

2. Enter the address of the computer you want to connect to.

3. Choose which services you want to use. File transfer allows you to access files on the hard drive. Remote control lets you control the mouse and access any resource on the computer, or a network, if the home PC is connected to a network. (See Figure 9.10.)

4. Click Connect.

Figure 9.9
Choose the Internet
connection feature in
LapLink

Figure 9.10
Select the services you
want and click OK

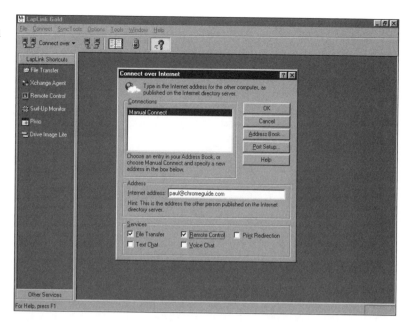

OTHER REMOTE CONTROL OPTIONS

GoToMyPC from ExpertCity is a Web-browser based service that allows you to remotely control a computer. The service is subscription based; you can sign up for a month or for a year. For more information, check out gotomypc.com.

Using Remote Desktop Connection in Windows XP

The Remote Desktop Connection feature of Windows XP has an obvious benefit: It's free. It also has a not-so-obvious drawback: You can only use it to connect to a PC running Windows XP Professional.

Most people who buy new computers probably use the less expensive version of XP—the Home edition. If you have a Windows XP Professional CD, you can use it to load Remote Desktop Connection onto computers running Windows 95 or later. Or, you can download it from: http://www.microsoft.com/windowsxp/remotedesktop/

Windows XP Home already has the Remote Desktop Connection software preinstalled. But, again, you can only use it to access a Windows XP Professional computer.

Remote Desktop Connection is a very handy application, if less feature-filled than LapLink and pcAnywhere remote access programs. Windows XP Home users, as well as

CHAPTER 9

users of other Windows operating systems, might instead check out the section, "Using Your Programs Remotely," for their remote access needs.

Before you can use Remote Desktop Connection, you need to set up the Windows XP Professional computer to accept the connection.

1. Choose Start > Settings > Control Panel, and double-click System.

2. From the Remote tab, choose "Allow users to connect remotely to this computer."

3. Click OK.

Now, when the XP Professional computer is ready to accept a connection, you can set up your remote computer to connect.

1. Install the program using a Windows XP Professional Disk or by downloading it from the site listed previously.

2. Select Start > Programs > Accessories > Communications > Remote Desktop Connection.

3. Choose the computer you want to access and click Connect (see Figure 9.11).

4. The Log On to Windows dialog box appears. Click OK.

5. Now, you should be able to see the desktop of the remote computer and use the programs and navigate through folders.

Figure 9.11

Connect to a Windows XP Professional PC

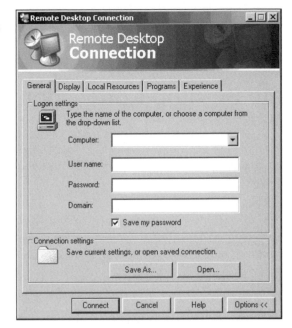

Remote Desktop Connection helps Windows XP Professional users get more out of their OS. It's too bad Microsoft didn't include Remote Desktop Connection in its Home edition, which more home users are obviously more likely to purchase. Those of us using Windows XP Home have good options in LapLink and pcAnywhere, but at an additional cost.

Dialing up Your Network from the Road

Now that you have your remote access setup working, consider a few tips before you hit the road. Your network is a wellspring of useful data, but it won't do you any good if you can't access it while you're traveling.

Keep the following tips in mind to remain in touch with your network.

▶ Make sure your computer is waiting. Most programs require that the program be running on the home PC so you can access it with your remote computer. LapLink and pcAnywhere have options for starting the programs automatically when Windows starts. It's a good idea to use them. If your computer at home is turned off or your remote access program isn't open, your $180 remote access program becomes useless.

▶ Test your setup before you leave. A remote access program might work great over your office network but leave you hanging when you try to dial up with a modem. Firewalls and routers can make remote access difficult. Firewalls and routers are designed to keep intruders out, but they'll also keep you out if you don't work around them. The support pages on your remote access program's Web site typically offer specific instructions on configuring routers and firewalls from different vendors.

▶ E-mail yourself a few files. As a precaution, send yourself contact files, a few important e-mails, and the project files you're currently working on. E-mail them to a free Web account like Yahoo or Hotmail, and you'll be in business even if you can't access your entire network from the road.

Using Your Programs Remotely

In addition to using remote access programs to connect to your network, you can use a free program that ships with Windows computers to control your computer from afar and share applications. NetMeeting (Start > Programs > Accessories > Communications > NetMeeting) offers a desktop-sharing feature that you can use to share applications remotely.

Set NetMeeting for program sharing on your home computer by following these directions.

1. Start NetMeeting. Tell NetMeeting to connect to a directory server, which helps users find each other. (You can also use this service to find your own computer.) Select Tools > Options and enter a server in the Directory

CHAPTER 9

text box. If you know the IP address of the computer to which you want to connect, you can skip this step and enter the IP address instead of using the directory service to find someone. We do that in the next set of steps.

2. Click the Share Program button, as shown in Figure 9.12.

3. Select the program you want to share (see Figure 9.13). If you click the Allow Control button, the remote user will be able to control your program.

4. The program you selected is available so that you can share it remotely.

Figure 9.12
Select the Share
Program button

Figure 9.13
Choose the program
you want to share

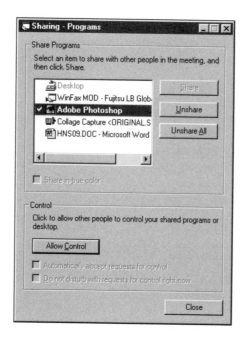

Though it doesn't offer as many features as LapLink and pcAnywhere, NetMeeting allows you to sign on to your unmanned computer. You need to set up a password first, and then quit NetMeeting on your home computer. The program leaves a small applet running (in your Windows system tray, in the right corner by the clock). This applet waits for requests and prompts the remote user for a password.

You can use the NetMeeting Remote Desktop feature on your remote computer by following these steps.

1. From NetMeeting, select Tools > Remote Desktop Sharing.
2. The Remote Desktop Sharing Wizard launches, as shown in Figure 9.14. Click Next.

3. Enter a password in both the New Password and Confirm New Password text boxes and then click Next. If it's the first time you've run the program, you won't be prompted for an old password. (See Figure 9.15.)

4. You can further secure your computer by choosing a password-protected screensaver, as shown in Figure 9.16.

5. When you finish the Wizard, exit NetMeeting. The program places an icon in your system tray.

6. Right-click the NetMeeting icon in your system tray and choose Activate Remote Desktop Sharing, as shown in Figure 9.17.

7. Call the computer you just configured, from the remote computer. Enter your password when prompted. You'll see the desktop of your home computer, which you can then control from your remote computer.

Figure 9.14
Follow the directions of the Remote Desktop Sharing Wizard

Figure 9.15
Enter a password to protect your home computer; remember your password—you'll need it when you want to access your computer remotely

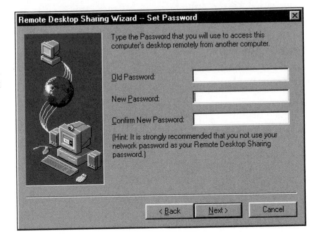

Figure 9.16
You can add another layer of protection by setting up a password-protected screensaver on the desktop of your home computer

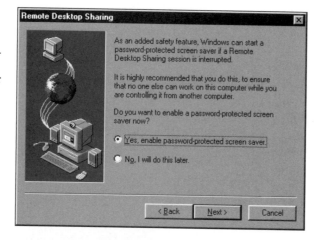

Figure 9.17
Activate NetMeeting by choosing Activate Remote Desktop Sharing

10

Security

Although important, securing your computer against hackers isn't something you should lose sleep over. There's always a level of risk involved with connecting your computer to the Internet, whether it's on a network or is a single PC dialing up to surf the Web. But you're not as attractive a target for an unscrupulous hacker as, say, NASA. However, you can take a few precautions that make your network harder to see, password-protected, and generally harder for a stranger to access.

First, a note on wireless networks. Wireless networks are inherently more insecure than wired networks. Because anyone within the range of your access point can gain access to your LAN, you need to take more precautions than you do with a wired network. Thankfully, protections are likely built-in to your wireless network card and access point (if you have one). You just need to use them. You'll find out how in this chapter.

Whether your network is wired or wireless, you should consider purchasing a router with a built-in firewall. This is an especially simple and cost effective way to quickly protect your network. A firewall hides your IP address from potential n'er-do-wells who scan IP addresses regularly looking for unprotected openings, sometimes called *backdoors*, to your network.

Some security measures you can take, such as blocking access to your PC with software or a hardware device called a firewall, or encrypting your e-mail, are useful both on PCs that connect directly to the Internet and on home networks. You can use these means to protect your data whether you have one PC or 100.

In addition, you should take steps to protect your network from viruses. You should install antivirus software and keep it updated. Thankfully, some of the personal firewall software we discuss in this chapter can help you limit the damage of some e-mail viruses.

Here's how to take care of business at home. These simple security measures help keep your network safe.

Why Worry about Security?

OK, so we understand that the threat of your network being hacked is something to take seriously but that you shouldn't be paranoid about it. The precautions you take to protect your computer and files should be equal to the level of threat. Some of the reasons why you want to make sure your network is secure are included in the following list.

> ▶ Hackers run programs that scan for IP addresses that are not protected. If they find an unprotected computer, they might try to access your files over the Internet. This is potentially more worrisome for those of us with "always-on" broadband connections that are available at all times. Firewalls can help.

> ▶ Radio waves pass through walls, and someone could access your network simply by stepping into range of your wireless network with a laptop that has a wireless network card. So, you need to make sure your wireless network is secure.

> ▶ Convenient features of Windows computing, such as file and printer sharing, on an unprotected computer on the Internet, are an invitation to muck around on your computer.

> ▶ From time to time, someone discovers a vulnerability in Windows that could be exploited. You should periodically download updates to your OS to keep it secure. We talk about periodic updates to Windows, and where you can download them, later in this chapter.

Wireless Is Inherently Less Secure

To hack into a wired network, you need some sort of physical connection to the network. That's not the case with wireless networks: Accessing a wireless network can be as simple as being in the proximity of a network adapter or access point. The radio signal from your wireless network adapter sends a signal about 150 feet (and more than twice that outdoors).

If you are concerned about someone accessing your data, enable WEP (Wired Equivalent Privacy), which encodes and decodes the information transferred over your wireless network (see Figure 10.1). We discuss enabling WEP later, in the section "Keeping Hackers Off Your Wireless Network."

Figure 10.1
WEP (Wired
Equivalent Privacy)
can act as a deterrent
to someone trying to
hack into your
wireless network

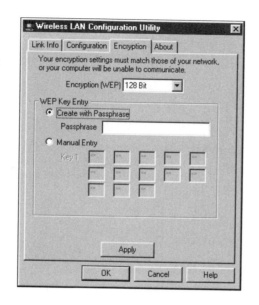

Broadband Connections Offer a Target for Hackers

Simply put, broadband connections are typically connected when your computer is on (rather than dialed up, as with a 56 kbps modem connection), so they're more likely to be hacked.

A hacker could, for example, access your computer and search through or delete your files. A hacker might access your computer to send out spam, or a virus, or simply use your identity to steal sensitive information, such as financial data or passwords, that you have stored on your computer. When your computer is connected to the Internet full-time, you increase your level of risk to unauthorized access. That's why cable and DSL modem connections are prime candidates for a hardware or software *firewall*. A firewall blocks unauthorized access to your PC over the Internet. A firewall can also check to make sure data sent from your computer is authorized. Some firewalls offer protection from viruses that send e-mails, for instance, from your address book, without you knowing it.

In my home, I use a firewall that's built-in my router. I also use a personal firewall called ZoneAlarm from Zone Labs (www.zonealarm.com) that's free for personal use. A commercial version of ZoneAlarm is also available—offering features, such as ad and cookie blocking—for $50.

SOFTWARE FIREWALLS
You can also buy software firewalls from Symantec (www.symantec.com) and McAfee (www.mcafee.com). These firewalls are effective, but I get along just fine with my free (for personal use) copy of ZoneAlarm from Zone Labs.

How to Protect Your Network

Now that we've identified some of the dangers, and talked a bit about what we can do about them, let's get to work protecting your network.

Hardware Firewall

First, let's consider a home network connected to a broadband modem. To get started, consider a firewall built-in your router. Many routers include firewalls, so you might as well make this an element of the deal.

A firewall built-in a router typically filters out unwanted data packets. A firewall can also monitor, and block, traffic going out from your network to the Internet. This can help avoid viruses that send unauthorized data from one of your computers, such as a rash of e-mails infected with a virus.

Most routers offer Network Address Translation (NAT). This feature allows the router to create a series of addresses that no one outside of your network can see. The router handles the request for Web pages and other Internet data, then forwards that data to the correct computer on your network. The one IP address your ISP provides you is shared by all the computers on your network. No one outside of your network knows that more than one computer is accessing the Internet.

Some firewalls act as a proxy server, accessing Web pages so that each page goes to the server instead of directly to each machine. The proxy server checks each request for data before it is sent out or received, and it creates a barrier between your computer and the Internet. Proxy servers can also cache pages, which means they are stored locally on the server. This allows for faster display of pages, because pages stored locally, on the server, can be delivered more quickly than if requested from your computer to a Web site.

Finally, some firewalls use stateful inspection. This means the firewall checks to make sure the data was requested from a user. If the data isn't the result of a request, it's blocked.

Software Firewall

Personal (software) firewalls protect one computer that connects to the Internet by dial-up 56 kbps or broadband modem. You can use personal firewalls, such as Zone Labs'

ZoneAlarm, Symantec Desktop Firewall, and McAfee.com Personal Firewall. Most personal firewalls act like proxy servers, checking data that goes in and out of your network and blocking unauthorized data packets.

Some personal firewalls offer features that protect you from Trojan horses—viruses that attempt to access the Internet without your permission or knowledge from your computer, such as the I Love You virus. An e-mail filter of this type is a very handy feature, and one you should look for when shopping for a personal firewall.

Software firewalls can also offer good protection to dial-up connections, which are less at risk than broadband connections, but still can be hacked.

If you use Windows XP, you already have a built-in, personal firewall within the operating system. Here's how to access it:

1. Open Network Connections from the Control Panel.

2. Right-click the connection you want to change (see Figure 10.2) and choose Properties from the shortcut menu.

3. Click the Advanced tab. Select the "Protect my computer and network by limiting or preventing access to this computer from the Internet" check box in the Internet Connection Firewall section, as shown in Figure 10.3. Click OK.

Figure 10.2
Right-click the connection you want to change

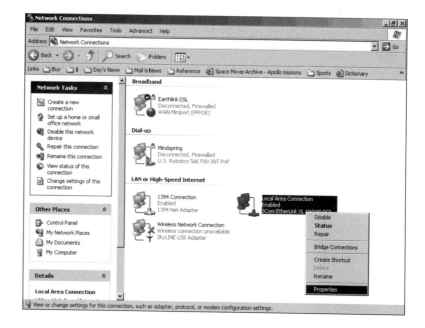

Figure 10.3
Enable the personal
firewall included in
Windows XP

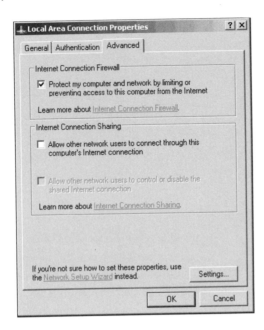

Not running Windows XP? That's OK. I can recommend a good personal firewall that's free for noncommercial use. You find out how to install the ZoneAlarm personal firewall later in this chapter (see Figure 10.4). See Table 10.1 for ideas on determining what type of firewall to install—depending on your system or network setup.

Figure 10.4
You can install a free
firewall program that
keeps programs from
accessing the Internet

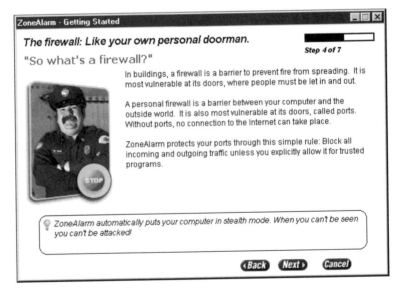

CAUTION

Firewalls can sometimes block access to computers *within* your network. You need to take steps to allow access to your networked computers. See the "Installing a Firewall Program" section for more information.

Table 10.1 Firewall Security	
If you have:	**Use:**
One PC connecting to the Internet via modem	A personal (a.k.a software) firewall, such as ZoneAlarm or the firewall feature of Windows XP.
A local area network (LAN) connecting multiple PCs by broadband modem	A firewall built into a router or a personal firewall on each machine.

Password Protect Folders

No matter what kind of network you use, you can make your data more difficult to hack by password protecting folders with sensitive information (see Figure 10.5). Also, use tough-to-guess passwords. When choosing a password, pick one you won't find in the dictionary, and use a combination of letters, numbers, and symbols.

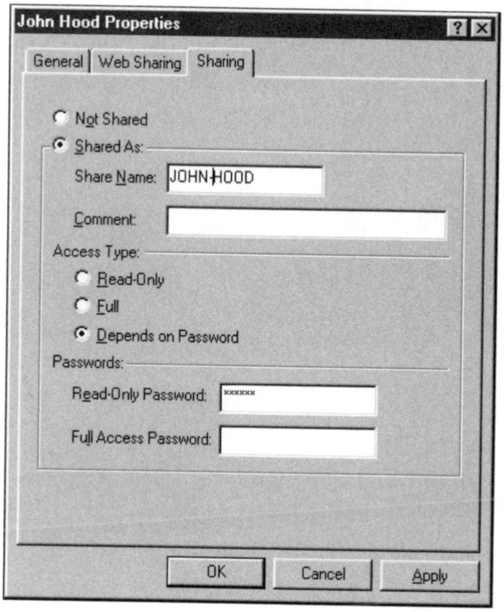

Figure 10.5
You can protect your folders by requiring a password

John Hood Properties dialog box showing the Sharing tab with options: Not Shared, Shared As (Share Name: JOHN HOOD, Comment: blank), Access Type (Read-Only, Full, Depends on Password selected), Passwords (Read-Only Password: ******, Full Access Password: blank). Buttons: OK, Cancel, Apply.

Download Updates

Even when you password protect folders, vulnerabilities in Windows can cause problems. A smart hacker can find ways to use these vulnerabilities to gain access to your system. Soon after Windows XP was released, for instance, a security hole was found that could allow a hacker to crash or take control of your system. How likely a scenario is that? Not terribly, but you should still keep an eye out for potential security problems with Windows.

One way you can minimize the risk is by downloading updates to Windows. You can download updates at: http://windowsupdate.microsoft.com.

Backup

The primary worry, whether you're concerned about bugs (programming glitches that cause programs to act unexpectedly) or hackers, is data loss. One way to deal with data loss before it happens is to back up your files. Backing up to a removable media, such as a Zip drive or rewritable CD, can give you peace of mind. And, if you unexpectedly lose data, you'll be sitting pretty.

We discuss backing up your network (see Figure 10.6) in detail in Chapter 11, "Troubleshooting."

Figure 10.6
Using Microsoft Backup, you can copy your files so that your data is protected

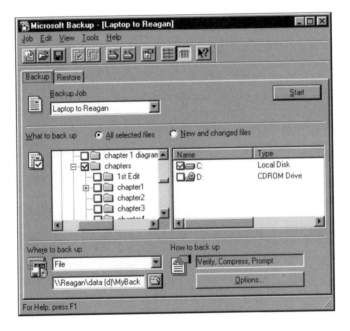

Data Encryption

Encryption encodes data so that even if someone should gain access to it, they won't be able to read and understand the data. We discuss enabling encryption for wireless networks a little later in the chapter. On any kind of network, including one PC dialing up an ISP to connect to the Internet, Pretty Good Privacy (PGP) can help protect your data from prying eyes.

Encryption is the process of using a secret code so that no one but the intended recipient can read your message. Encryption is typically done by scrambling the data in your message and combining it with a binary number, called a key, to make the data unreadable. The message can only be decoded if your recipient has the key.

Of course, any code, with the right amount of brainpower and time, can be broken. However, encryption is certainly a much safer way to send sensitive information over the Internet. PGP is one of the most popular means of encrypting e-mail. PGP uses public key cryptography, which requires two keys. You use someone's public key to send them a message. The recipient uses their private key to decode the message. The two keys are called a key pair. You can protect individual files, or e-mails, by highlighting the file or e-mail and instructing PGP (through an icon in your system tray) to encrypt the data.

You can find out more about PGP, and download a free version, at www.pgpi.com or http://www.pgp.com/products/freeware.

A simpler way to send encrypted e-mail is to use an online service that encrypts the mail for you. One such service is ZixMail (www.zixmail.com). You can download a 2 MB file that encrypts your mail as you send it. Your recipient also needs ZixMail installed on his or her computer. The service is offered free if you have a Yahoo mail account (also free).

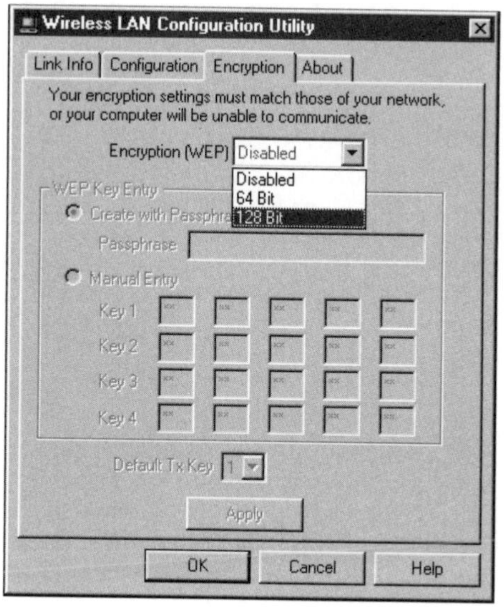

Figure 10.7
You can enable encryption on your wireless network card

Installing a Firewall Program

Several good firewall programs are available. Some firewall software is even free for personal use, and as mentioned before, Windows XP comes with a built-in firewall that you can access from the Network Connections Control Panel.

ZoneAlarm is a handy program, particularly because it can work with networks. You do have to make a change to the program to allow it do so, however. If you don't, ZoneAlarm does its job: It keeps computers from accessing your PC, even if they're on your LAN.

You can download the program by visiting Zone Lab's Web site (www.zonelabs.com) with your browser.

Note that firewalls can also create problems accessing computers from within your LAN. You might need to adjust the settings on your firewall to allow the computers on your LAN to access each other. If you use ZoneAlarm, for example, you can set up the software so that it allows access to PCs on your network.

1. Open ZoneAlarm.

2. Click the Advanced button (see Figure 10.8).

3. Under "Adapter Subnets," select the name of your network card (see Figure 10.9). This provides access to the other computers on your network.

4. Click OK.

Figure 10.8
Software firewalls can actually block access to the PCs on your own network: It's important to configure ZoneAlarm, for instance, to identify computers on your network that should be allowed access to each other

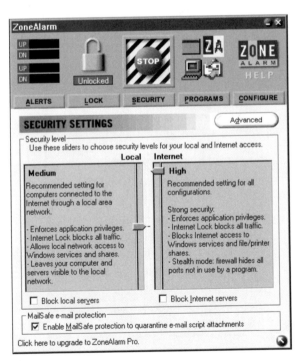

Figure 10.9
You can change the
ZoneAlarm settings
to allow access to
computers on
your network

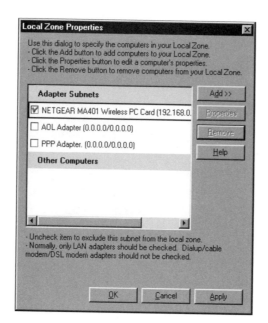

Keeping Hackers Off Your Wireless Network

To keep unwanted users off your wireless network, you should typically take two
precautions.

▶ Enable encryption (WEP)

▶ Use a firewall on each PC

Typically, I do not use encryption, because the work necessary to encrypt data actually
slows the network by 10 to 20 percent. I use a wireless router with a firewall, so I have
protection from threats that might attempt to attack my computer over the Internet. However, if my neighbor decides to log on to my network from his driveway, he probably can.
That's a level of risk I'm comfortable accepting. You should let the sensitivity of your data
drive the level of precautionary measures you take. Worried about someone accessing your
network from the parking lot? Use encryption. The greater the sensitivity/threat, the
greater the level of encryption you should use.

The Service Set Identifier (SSID) is a string of text that identifies your network and must be
entered into the configuration software for each adapter or access point (see Figure 10.10).
The SSIDs all need to match, but this data can be "sniffed" or accessed surreptitiously over
the airwaves by a smart hacker, so it doesn't provide any real security except to keep cheap-
skate neighbors from secretly hogging your bandwidth.

Figure 10.10

Set the SSID on a
wireless network

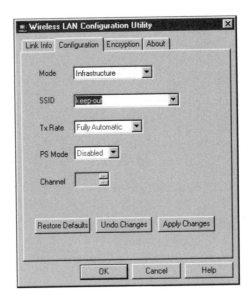

As discussed throughout this chapter, a firewall can block access from intruders by hiding your IP address. If someone should try to access your wireless network by coming into range of your network with a wireless network card, a personal firewall installed on each PC can block access. Just remember to provide access to PCs on your network, and block all other access.

Safe computing to you.

11

Troubleshooting

Getting a network started is the hard part. Keeping your network running should be easy. You'll invariably run into problems from time to time, however. In this chapter, we look at some ways to get out of a pinch—for instance, if you can't find a computer on the network. We also look at how to prevent some avoidable hassles by, for example, installing current antivirus software to protect your network.

If you're setting up a very simple network, with just a couple of computers and some Ethernet cable, you'll probably have less trouble than if you're setting up a wireless network with ten computers connecting to a hub, a router, and a broadband modem. The more complex the network, the more time you need to invest to keep it operating properly.

Wireless networks add a level of complication because they involve radio transceivers for communicating, which take more time to set up than most wired network hardware. In addition, wireless networks have a certain range over which they can send a signal. As you move farther away from a wireless network adapter or access point, transmission speed drops off. Get far enough away, even indoors, usually beyond 150 feet, and you get no signal at all.

As with most things technical, the hang-ups you'll face are often simple to correct. Check your cables to make sure they're securely plugged in, and check the green lights on your network cards to see if there is network activity. A lost network connection could be caused by something as simple as a loose cable, or it could be as problematic, and disappointing, as a wireless network adapter that is on the fritz and needs to go back to the manufacturer.

Find Your Network When Your PC Can't

One of the most frustrating network problems is trying to find a computer in Network Neighborhood (Windows 95/98) or My Network Places (Windows Me, 2000, or XP) and not seeing a computer that you *know* is connected. Here are a few quick ideas to get you started diagnosing the problem:

▶ Log off Windows and log on again (see Figure 11.1). First, try this with the computer that isn't appearing on the network. Then, try logging off and on again from the computer you are using to try to access another PC on the network. Windows won't recognize your computer on the network if you haven't logged on (for instance, if you press the Esc key instead of clicking the OK button when the Windows logon dialog box appears at startup).

▶ If you have firewall software on your PC, turn the software off temporarily to see if that's the problem. If it is, you need to configure your firewall to allow access to all the PCs on your network. That means changing your firewall software on each PC on your network. Refer to your firewall's help documentation for assistance with this.

▶ When you first install a wireless network, disable encryption temporarily before you get everything installed. After your network is up and running, you can then enable encryption at each computer and at the access point using the configuration software that comes with your wireless network card.

▶ Make sure, especially on Windows 95 and 98 computers, that you have Microsoft File and Printer Sharing enabled—both on the computer you are using and the one you are trying to access over the network. From your desktop, right-click Network Neighborhood and choose Properties. Make sure File and Printer Sharing for Microsoft Networks is in the list of installed components. If not, click the File and Printer Sharing button (see Figure 11.2). Select "I want to be able to give others access to my files." Click OK twice to close the open dialog boxes, then restart the computer when prompted.

▶ When all else fails, reboot. You'd be surprised how many times this clears up a disappearing act.

Figure 11.1
Choose Log Off from
the Start menu, and
then log on again to
make sure your PC
appears on the network

Figure 11.2
Make sure File and
Printer Sharing is
enabled

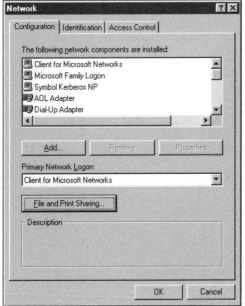

Here's another tip, if you're having trouble seeing your networked computers in Network Neighborhood. In Windows 95 and 98 networks, in particular, you might see this problem, which can be caused by hardware and software conflicts. Try installing NetBIOS over IPX on each PC. NetBIOS (Network Basic Input Output System) is software that allows programs to share data between networked computers. IPX (Internetwork Packet eXchange) is a protocol used to deliver data across networks. Most people don't need to install NetBIOS over IPX to share files on their LAN, but it can be a useful protocol to install when you're having difficulty with your network.

Make sure your Windows 98 disk in is the drive.

1. Right-click Network Properties.

2. Click Add.

3. Choose Protocol.

4. Click Add.

5. Scroll down to Microsoft.

6. Select IPX/SPX-compatible Protocol.

7. Double-click the IPX protocol under the list of installed network components.

8. Select "I want to enable NetBIOS over IPX/SPX."

9. Click OK twice to close the open dialog boxes.

10. Windows copies the files from the Windows 98 CD. When prompted, click OK to restart your computer.

If this tip doesn't work for you, you can remove the protocol: It won't foul up your system.

1. Right-click Network Neighborhood and choose Properties.

2. Click the Configuration tab (if it's not already selected).

3. Look under the list "The following network components are installed."

4. Select "NetBIOS support for the IPX/SPX protocol." Click Remove.

5. Click OK to save your changes.

6. You are prompted to restart your computer. Click OK to reboot.

FINDING OTHER COMPUTERS ON YOUR NETWORK
You can find other computers on your network from the Run menu. Click Start > Run, and in the Open box, type:
\\(name of computer)
Then, click the OK button. The shared folders and printers should appear in a Windows Explorer menu.
You can also find computers by clicking Start > Run, and then typing net view in the Open text box.
You'll see a list of the computers in your network. If you are not logged on, you might not see computers on your network, and you'll be prompted to reboot.

Using Windows 98 and 2000 Together

One common problem in mixed-operating system environments is the password requirement of Windows 2000. Many folks end up using Windows 98 and 2000 computers in the
same office. Unless you set up Windows 2000 to allow access to Windows 98 PCs, you
won't be able to share files and folders on a Windows 2000 machine.

Mixing Windows 98 and 2000 is a common situation, but it can lead to difficulty if you
don't set things up correctly. If you have a Windows 2000 computer on your network, you
need to give a username and password to each person on your network.

1. From the Windows 2000 computer, click Start > Settings > Control Panel
    and open Users and Passwords. Click Add. (See Figure 11.3.)

2. Type in a name. Click Next, then enter a password. Click the Next button.

3. Decide whether to allow the user to install programs on the Windows 2000
    machine. If you don't want this feature, choose Restricted User. Most
    often, you use the Standard User settings, which is the default choice.

4. Click Finish.

You are prompted to enter a password each time you try to access a Windows 2000 computer, whether or not you've established a password on the Windows 2000 computer.
Now, you know what to enter to access the Windows 2000 computer when prompted. In
addition, you now have access to the Windows 2000 PC's shared resources that you can
access through Network Neighborhood from your computer.

Figure 11.3
Add a username and
password to a
Windows 2000
machine

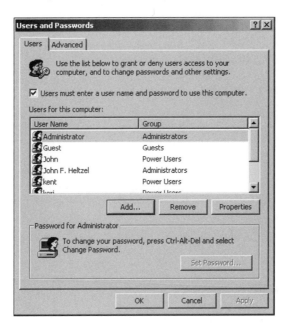

CHAPTER 11

Common Mistakes and Problems

Networks can be picky. If things aren't set just right, you might think something very serious has happened to your equipment or your software. The trouble is often something simple. In most cases, your network acts up because of some small thing you did or didn't do. You might not be able to access the Internet. Or, a PC that showed up in Network Neighborhood (or My Network Places, if you use Windows Me/2000/XP) yesterday isn't showing up today. It could be as simple as a button that needs to be pushed on a hub (or toggled off).

The information in Table 11.1 is based on dumb mistakes I've made setting up networks for businesses and for myself when I test equipment.

Sometimes, believe it or not, the problem isn't your fault. I've also got a few ideas to fix common problems that are not self-inflicted.

Table 11.1 Common Problems and the First Place to Check	
Problem	**Check:**
No Link light	Make sure cables are connected. In wireless networks, make sure the channel, SSID, and mode (infrastructure or ad-hoc) are the same at each PC and at the access point, if you have one.
Computer doesn't appear in Network Neighborhood/ My Network Places	Make sure, especially on Windows 95/98 systems, that you're logged on to the network (don't press Esc at the logon screen at startup). If you have a software firewall installed on your PCs, turn off the firewall first and make sure that's not the problem. If it is, you need to use the vendor's instructions to make the firewall aware of the PCs on your network. (Note: Not all personal firewalls are capable of running on a LAN.)
No Internet access	Restart your cable or DSL modem, then restart your router, in that order. If your router doesn't have a restart button, unplug it, wait a few seconds, then plug it back in.

Firewall Hang-Ups

We're talking about personal, software firewalls here, not the kind that are built-in to a router. Leaving a firewall on when you don't mean to or when you haven't yet configured it to work on your LAN (see Chapter 10, "Security") can stop your network cold. Your PC might connect to the Internet, but it won't show up on your network. Before you attempt to access files on your network, disable your firewall. Then, after things are chugging along, turn the firewall on and set your firewall to recognize the PCs on your LAN. (Check your software's instructions for this and, obviously, make sure your personal firewall is one that supports network use. Most, but not all, do.)

Figure 11.4
If you use the built-in firewall feature of Windows XP (or another software firewall), turn off the firewall when setting up your network; you can turn it back on, then run the Network Setup Wizard, once your network is up and running

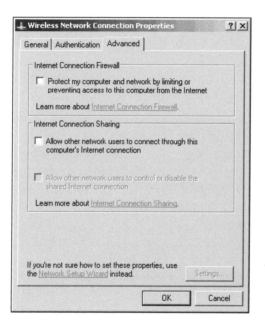

Check Your Hub

Here's the problem: Your computers are all connected to a hub and they're working fine. All of a sudden, nothing's working. You can't reach the Internet from any of the computers. You can't share files or printers. What happened?

If your hub has an "uplink" or "crossover" button, try toggling it. Hubs sometimes come with a button that lets you use a crossover or a straight-through cable to connect one hub to another. The uplink button should be turned off if you're using a straight-through cable to connect one hub to another. If it's not, your hub won't be able to communicate with the other hub, and your network won't work. These buttons are easy to accidentally toggle.

Along the same lines, some routers have crossover or uplink buttons. Toggle them if your network stops responding to see if that fixes the problem.

Check Your Cabling

A disconnected cable can cause unnecessary heartbreak. Look for the green "Link" light on the back of Ethernet network adapter cards. Almost all network adapters, wired and wireless, have a green light to show that you have a connection to your LAN. It should stay lit. Often, another green light blinks on and off to show that there's activity on the network. If your Link light is dark, your cable might be unplugged. If the cable is secure, make sure your card is installed correctly and that you have up-to-date drivers installed.

Discard any cables that have broken connectors or are otherwise prone to become disconnected.

Viruses

Another self-inflicted problem: Viruses. If you take precautions, you can keep your network virus-free. Sadly, viruses are able to spread quickly on networks. E-mail from co-workers often seems safe, but could quickly spread a virus throughout your LAN.

Make sure that you have virus detection software installed. Your antivirus software should check e-mail attachments when they arrive, and before they're opened.

Never open an attachment that you're not familiar with. In addition, make sure your antivirus software has a recent definition list (see Figure 11.5). Definition lists make sure your antivirus software is aware of viruses that are currently circulating, sometimes referred to as being *in the wild.*

Most antivirus software now comes with an automated feature that connects to the Internet and downloads the latest definition lists. Make sure you use this feature.

Figure 11.5
Make sure your virus definition lists are up-to-date to keep viruses from infecting your network

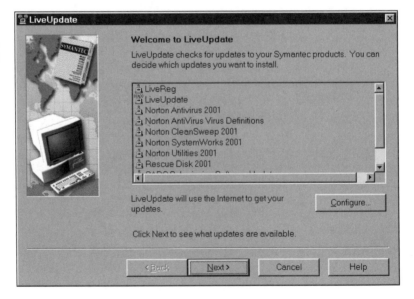

RESET YOUR BROADBAND INTERNET CONNECTION

When your broadband Internet connection is down, and you can't browse the Web or send e-mail from any of your machines, try this: First, reset the modem. Make sure your power and connection lights are lit on the cable or DSL modem. Then, reset your router. Sometimes, your modem needs to make a request for a new IP address, and this might cause your network to lose its Internet access temporarily. Resetting the modem, then the router, often fixes odd connection problems.

Backing Up Your Network

Backing up is one of those upkeep tasks you figure you'll get around to sooner or later. Something always comes up, or it just seems like too much of a hassle. But really, backing up your important files isn't that big a deal, and the software for backup is built-in to Windows.

Windows 95/98

The smartest way to back up is to save your files to removable media, such as an Iomega Zip or tape drive. That way, you can take your backup with you or store it off-site, which provides greater security.

Personally, I just don't have a need for removable media beyond a CD-drive. If there's a fire at my house or if, for some other reason, all my computers go down at once, I'm in trouble. But that's a level of risk I'm willing to accept. Sometimes, I use rewritable CDs, but they don't have the storage capacity necessary to hold the information on even one of my hard drives. Instead, I usually back up to another machine on my network using Microsoft Backup. Microsoft Backup also compresses the files as it backs them up, saving disk space.

Here's how to back up your system with Microsoft Backup:

1. Click Start > Programs > Accessories > System Tools > Backup.
2. Choose "Create a new backup job" and click OK, as shown in Figure 11.6.
3. Choose whether you want to do a full or partial backup. Personally, I prefer to back up the files I select to save time and space. I back up folders on my root drive (usually the "C" drive), such as My Documents, and /Windows/Favorites, /Windows/Application Data folder, as well as my e-mail.
4. Select the files you want to back up.
5. Choose where you want to store the files.
6. Continue answering the Backup Wizard questions, then click Start to begin the backup.

Figure 11.6
Start a new backup job
with Microsoft Backup

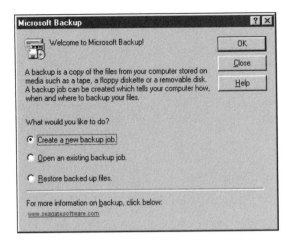

Windows XP System Restore

Although Windows XP does not include Microsoft Backup, it does include a utility that can be really helpful. If you should run into a problem that you can't figure out, you can restore your system to the way it was working at an earlier time. If your computer was working fine before, you should be looking good after a system restore.

THE IMPORTANCE OF REGULAR BACKUPS

System Restore is an incredibly helpful new utility, but it won't replace the security of regular data backups. Windows XP Home does not offer the backup utility on the default installation, but you can add it from your Windows XP Home CD (it's in the /valueadd folder). Microsoft Backup is installed by default in Windows XP Professional.

After your computer is up and running on your network, consider creating a *restore point*, or a point in time in which your system is working correctly. The utility makes a snapshot of your system files at the point in time you choose. You can restore the system to a state in which it was working correctly, without losing data, such as e-mails and files you've created since that time. Here's how to create a restore point in Windows XP:

1. Choose Start > All Programs > Accessories > System Tools > System Restore.

2. Click "Create a restore point" and then click Next.

3. Enter a name to identify your restore point, then click "Create."

SYSTEM RESTORE VS. SYSTEM RESOURCES

System Restore eats up a lot of hard drive space. It can be a real lifesaver, but it munches your hard drive. A recent restore I created took up more than 700 MB. No big deal on a 40 GB hard drive, but a bit too much to ask when disk space is running tight.

If something should go wrong and you can't get your computer back on your network, you can load the restore point that you set in the previous set of steps. To restore your system, follow these steps.

1. Open the System Restore utility (Start > All Programs > Accessories > System Tools > System Restore).

2. Select Create a restore point, and then click the Next button.

3. Select an available restore point from the list that appears (see Figure 11.7).

4. Click Next.

Figure 11.7
Create a backup of your system, as it is today (hopefully working) so you can bring your system back to life, care of the System Restore utility, found in Windows XP

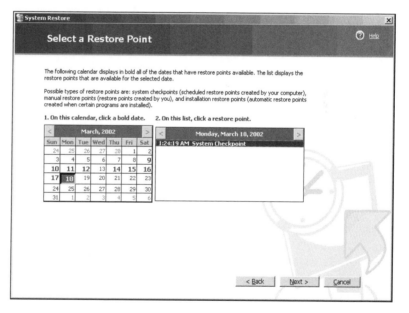

CHAPTER 11

12

Upgrading

In this chapter, you'll learn about ways to expand and upgrade your network.

Up until recently, the only networking technology available was Ethernet, so you'll see quite a bit of that technology on your broadband modem, on routers, and on PCs that ship with network cards, whether or not you plan to use Ethernet for your home network. Most home network technologies, such as phoneline and wireless, offer ways to connect to Ethernet equipment, such as hubs and cable/DSL modems. Among networking hardware, Ethernet is the utility player.

In the future, we'll see new, faster wireless equipment. Some of these technologies will work well together and some will not. It's important to shop around before you buy, to avoid equipment that might be a bad fit for your home or home office down the line, as you continue to build and improve your network.

We also look at whether you might find use in your home network for a computer that provides access to (or *serves)* files, programs, and printers to everyone on your network. If you think a server might help you, you can set up an old computer you have lying around the house to act as your server.

Making Sure You've Got Room to Grow

You might be tempted, when shopping for equipment, to buy just what you need at the time. In general, though, buying a bit more than you think you'll need down the line is useful. You should keep a few considerations in mind as you shop, so that you'll be able to easily upgrade later.

Hubs

When shopping for Ethernet hubs (see Figure 12.1), keep in mind that you might need more ports than you think. If you add a computer later, or decide to sign up for broadband Internet access and its accompanying cable or DSL modem, you'll need additional ports to connect your hardware.

That said, you can connect one hub to another, so that provides an upgrade option. But, as a rule of thumb, buy a hub that has more ports than you think you need. You want to be able to add more computers to your LAN without adding more networking equipment if you can help it. Remember to reserve enough ports for an Ethernet printer (if you have one), a broadband modem, and the number of computers you currently own.

For more upgrade options, see Table 12.1.

Figure 12.1
A hub from Netgear—when in doubt, buy a hub with a few more ports than you think you'll need

Table 12.1 Upgrade Options	
If you need to:	**Then add:**
Connect more PCs by Ethernet	A new hub
Connect wireless and wired PCs	An access point
Mix phoneline and Ethernet hardware	A phoneline to Ethernet bridge
Mix powerline and Ethernet hardware	A powerline to Ethernet bridge

Wireless Equipment

Wireless equipment throws a few tricky purchasing decisions your way. Competing standards and upcoming technologies can make buying equipment a little confusing. Thankfully, a good, reasonably-priced wireless technology, 802.11b (or Wi-Fi) is now available.

802.11b is Not Going Anywhere Soon

One of the reasons 802.11b is a good choice for the future is that the technology—despite being slower than upcoming technologies such as 802.11a, which is about five times faster than 802.11b—has widespread acceptance and is used in many businesses and homes. That means workers can set up their home networks, then connect to a corporate network at the office. In addition, travelers will find more and more public LANs that use 802.11b technology. Many airports, Starbucks coffee shops, hotels, conference centers, and other businesses are currently rolling out 802.11b service.

Public Access Wireless

Public access wireless is an area of wireless computing that's growing quickly. If you travel often, and have a wireless network card, public wireless local area networks (WLANs) can provide you with broadband speed on the go.

An interesting new company is Boingo (see Figure 12.2). The company lets you search by location to find where they have installed public wireless 802.11b access (as shown in Figure 12.3). You can find more information at www.boingo.com.

Figure 12.2
Boingo offers public access to wireless networks around the country

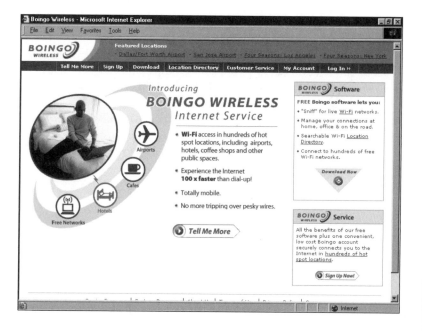

Figure 12.3
You can search for an
802.11b public
network using the
Boingo Web site; you
can search by state and
city for a location near
where you'll be
traveling

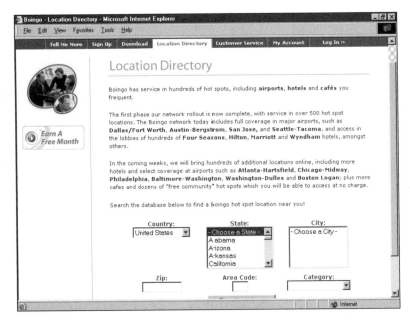

MobileStar (www.mobilestar.com) is another company providing wireless Internet access, at about $30 a month, at airports, coffee shops, and hotel lounges. As shown in Figure 12.4, you can also search for locations through MobileStar's Web site.

Figure 12.4
Finding locations at
MobileStar: The states
highlighted (in blue)
currently offer service

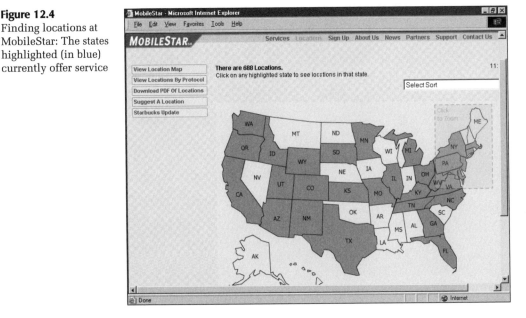

Wayport (www.wayport.com), yet another provider, offers public LAN access, wirelessly, at airports and hotels. Figure 12.5 shows Wayport's location finder.

Figure 12.5
Waypoint offers places to connect to an 802.11b network for Internet access, in the United States and abroad

All of these companies' Web sites offer a search feature that allows you to see if a wireless LAN is in your area, or at hotels, airports, or coffee shops where you plan to be in the future. In a nutshell, 802.11b is a good choice because it's prevalent.

Further wireless standards, such as the very fast 802.11a, won't be compatible with the current generation of Wi-Fi equipment. But it's clear that 802.11b isn't going anywhere soon, so you can buy into this technology with confidence. In addition, 802.11a dual-mode equipment, which includes an 802.11b access point, are planned, so that you can use the two technologies in the same home or office, even if they can't communicate directly.

Mixing Equipment

One way you can extend the range and usefulness of your network is to mix different types of network hardware. For example, you can mix powerline, phoneline, or Ethernet networking equipment to extend the distance of your wireless network. Likewise, you can add a wireless access point to an Ethernet network, so that you can take your laptop around the house wirelessly. In either case, a simple piece of equipment called a *bridge* can help. A bridge allows you to access one network using two or more technologies (powerline and Ethernet, for example).

Let's say you have two computers connected by Ethernet, and you want to add another computer upstairs (in a room with a phone jack) to the network. Instead of stringing cable to the computer upstairs, use a phoneline bridge. Here's an example of how you could go about it:

1. Plug one end of the phoneline-to-Ethernet bridge (see Figure 12.6) into your Ethernet hub.

2. Plug the other end of the bridge into a regular phone wall jack.

3. Connect a phoneline network adapter to your computer upstairs.

Figure 12.6
A phoneline to Ethernet bridge from Linksys (Photo courtesy of the Linksys Group, Inc. 2002)

What if you don't have a phone jack in the room where you want to add a new computer to your network? You can use a powerline-to-Ethernet bridge so that you can add a computer in any room with an outlet.

Wireless access points (see Figure 12.7), as we've discussed earlier in the book, also act as a bridge, allowing Ethernet equipment, such as a cable or DSL modem, to connect to a wireless network.

Figure 12.7
An 802.11a access point—in late 2002, models are expected that will also contain an 802.11b radio transmitter/receiver; the two technologies are incompatible, but the additional radio will allow 802.11a and 802.11b equipment to access the same network

Finally, you can use USB-to-Ethernet adapters to connect a broadband modem or any other Ethernet-based equipment to a computer that has a USB port but no Ethernet network card.

Networks that mix home networking technologies are often called *hybrid* networks, and they can make your LAN much more effective and useful.

How a Server Can Help You

A server can help by centralizing some of the tasks that you need to accomplish each day. For instance, a computer set up as a file and printer server allows everyone in your home access to one printer.

Servers are the heart of many office networks, allowing many users to access the same resources from one shared computer (and in some cases, many servers are used to share large amounts of data). Servers can be used to share applications (such as Lotus Notes), files (pictures or word processing documents, for example), or to manage Internet access on a network.

Because Windows offers built-in networking software, much of the usefulness found in an office server is already built into your PCs. A server can be helpful in small office environments, but most home networks won't use a server. Home networks typically allow the computers to connect to each other directly (a setup or configuration called *peer-to-peer*) rather than communicating through a server (*client-server*).

Most often, a server is the fastest computer in the building, with the largest hard drive or hard drives. But, you can turn any computer into a server. (See Figure 12.8.) Here are a few things you can do with a server in your home.

▶ A server speeds up your work. Each time you access a computer on your network to open or copy a file, you add a drain to the resources available to the computer you are accessing. Designating one computer as a server lets you grab files at will without slowing any one person down.

▶ You can install programs from a server. Have a handful of programs or drivers that you install often? Load them onto your server. Then, each computer has access to these programs and drivers, and can install them directly from the server, instead of hunting for CDs or floppies.

▶ Install a printer on your server and keep a copy of the printer drivers, including ones for different operating systems, on the server for easy access. Your printouts go to a central location, rather than to someone's desk.

Figure 12.8
A rack of powerful PowerEdge servers from Dell; office networks often use powerful, high-end machines to serve applications and files to workers on the network, but, at home, you can set up a simple file server with an extra PC—it doesn't need to be the fastest machine you've got, because your demands on the server will be minimal

Share Data

You can set aside one computer on your network to act as your file server. File servers act as a storing place for data that folks in your home (or home office) need to share.

Connect a Printer

Connect your printer to a server, and let everyone print to that PC (see Figure 12.9). Now, no one person in your office has to view the error messages when a file poops out. Another benefit: Some standalone printer servers don't support USB printers. If your server has USB ports, you're in business for sharing a USB printer. You can always share any printer connected to your network; in some cases, especially in a home office, having your best printer centralized can provide easier access to everyone on your network.

Figure 12.9
Connect an old PC to your printer, then have each person in your house add the network printer to their systems

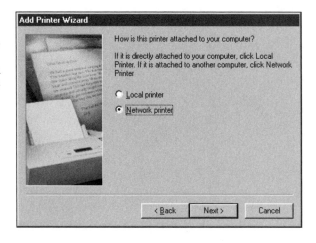

Share a CD-ROM or Scanner

Connect the peripherals everyone in your home uses—scanner, CD burner, or (soon) a DVD burner—to one computer. Each person can access the peripherals and save files to the server, as shown in Figure 12.10.

Figure 12.10
Share programs you install often, such as drivers, on a server

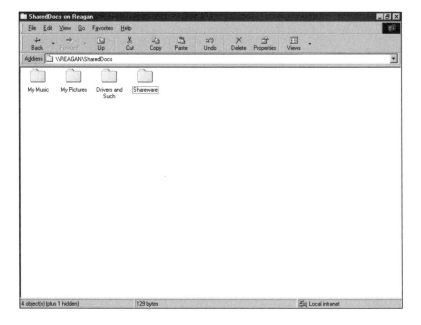

Connect a File Server to Your Network

Connecting a server is simple. Set up the computer you're going to use as your server (if it's not already) and follow these steps:

1. Install your network card.

2. Connect your server to the hub, or if the server is connected wirelessly, install and configure the software that came with your wireless network card.

3. Name your computer. (See Figure 12.11.) The name should make it clear that this machine is the server.

4. Give the server the same workgroup name that the other computers on your LAN are using.

Figure 12.11
Name your server so others on your home network can find it

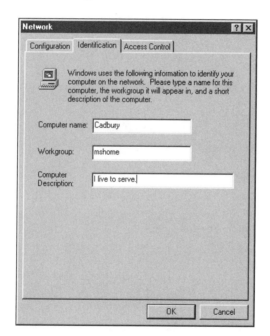

To start File and Print Sharing, see Chapter 5, "Sharing Data and Equipment."

Set Up a Simple Intranet

Windows 98 comes with the Personal Web server on the Windows 98 CD-ROM. Here's how to load it on to your system and share an inter-office Web site (or intranet) at your house or home office. First, put your Windows 98 disk in your CD-ROM drive (if the Windows 98 splash screen opens up, click Browse This CD button and skip Steps 1 and 2). If the splash screen does not appear, start at Step 1.

1. Open My Computer.
2. Double-click the icon of your CD drive.
3. Open the folder \add-ons\pws (see Figure 12.12).
4. Double-click setup.exe.
5. Click OK.
6. Click Next, then click the Add/Remove button.

The Personal Web Server Setup screen appears. Click Next and follow the wizard's instructions (see Figure 12.13).

Figure 12.12
Windows 98 users can install the Personal Web Server from Microsoft—it's included free on the Windows 98 disk

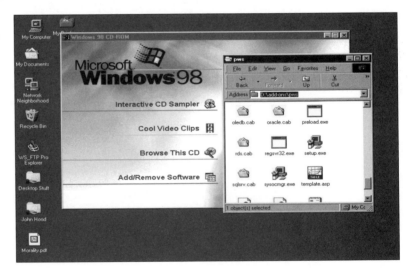

Figure 12.13
Follow the Personal
Web Server setup

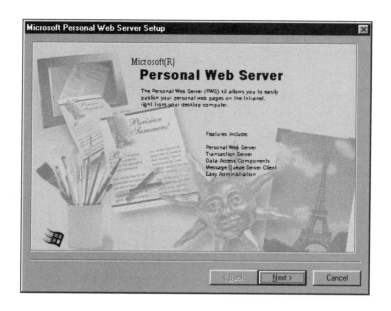

Setting up an intranet is a book in itself. However, you can actually find quite a bit of information on creating an intranet in the documentation for the Personal Web Server and in the FrontPage Express application, which is included with Microsoft Internet Explorer.

Sadly, Windows XP Home does not include a Web server. You'll need XP Professional for that. However, you can run the free Apache Web server on XP home (but note that it's a bit more difficult to set up than the Personal Web Server that comes with Windows 98).

FINDING THE APACHE WEB SERVER
For more information about, or to download, the Apache Web server, check out: www.apache.org.

CHAPTER 12

13

Windows XP Case Study

In this chapter, you combine everything you've learned so far in this book and follow a step-by-step approach to connect a computer to a small network, and to the Internet, using a broadband modem.

For this case study, we start with a computer running the latest operating system from Microsoft, Windows XP (Home edition). Windows XP Professional also includes the Network Setup Wizard, which we'll use to share files and printers, as well as Internet access. We also connect Windows Me and 98 computers, using the setup disk we create using Windows XP. The disk makes setup simpler on the other machines and automates a few steps, including the configuration of TCP/IP settings.

The computers will connect through a broadband modem, shared by the Windows XP system, for Internet access. The connection is shared through Windows Internet Connection Sharing (a software router bundled free in Windows 98 Second Edition and later operating systems).

We assume that you have all your equipment connected. You'll need a network adapter for each computer you want to connect. You can use wireless network adapters, no-new-wires network adapters (such as phoneline and powerline), or Ethernet. Just make sure all your hardware is connected before following these steps.

Start the Network Setup Wizard

The best part of this process is that we're going to let the Windows XP Network Setup Wizard handle most of the grunt work for us. The Network Setup Wizard handles configuring network adapters, naming the computer, starting file sharing and Internet sharing, and, most importantly, creating a networking disk we can use on our non-Windows XP systems to configure them. Let's get started.

In our example, we start with the computer that will share its connection, using ICS. Launch the Network Setup Wizard. Choose Start > All Programs > Accessories > Communications > Network Setup Wizard, as shown in Figure 13.1.

Figure 13.1
Start the Network
Setup Wizard

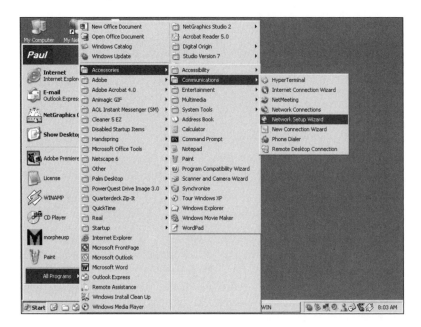

ALTERNATIVE WAYS TO ACCESS THE NETWORK SETUP WIZARD
You can also start the Network Setup Wizard by choosing Start > Settings > Control Panel and double-clicking Network Connections. Under Common Tasks, click Network Setup Wizard.

The Network Setup Wizard screen opens (as shown in Figure 13.2). This screen tells you that you can set up the following services:

▶ Internet Connection Sharing

▶ An Internet firewall

▶ File Sharing

▶ Printer sharing

Click Next to continue.

Figure 13.2
The Network Setup Wizard splash screen welcomes you to the world of networking

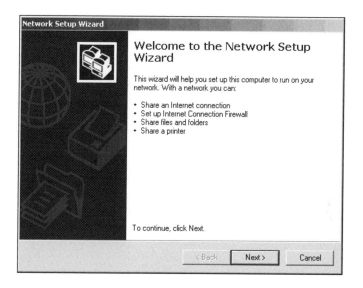

The next screen encourages you to consider a setup checklist. If you're interested in some pre-setup advice, click the "checklist for creating a network" link, as shown in Figure 13.3.

Figure 13.3
Click the checklist link for some pre-installation network tips from Windows XP

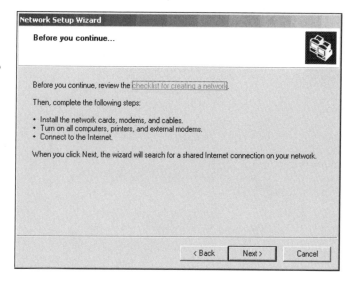

The checklist is essentially a Web page that offers different setup tips based on options you choose, which relate to the type of network you plan to create (see Figure 13.4). When you're done, close the checklist and you'll see the Network Setup Wizard dialog box is still open. If you plan to share an Internet connection, as we do in this example, make sure you are connected to the Internet. Click Next.

Figure 13.4
The network setup checklist offers software and hardware tips, as well as buying advice, for sharing files and Internet access

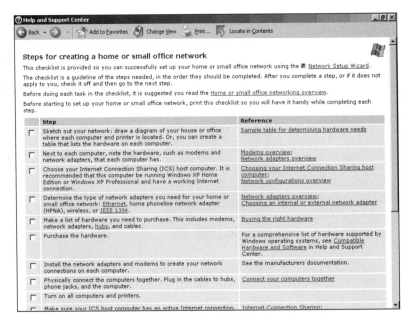

If you have network hardware that isn't connected, you'll see a screen asking you to either connect the hardware or select the option "Ignore disconnected network hardware," as shown in Figure 13.5. To proceed, click Next.

Figure 13.5
If you have hardware that's disconnected, connect it, or tell Windows XP that it's not being used by selecting "Ignore disconnected network hardware"

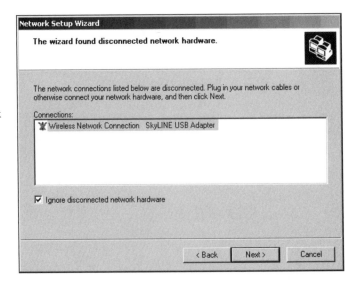

Now, you choose how your computer connects to the Internet. In this example, the Windows XP machine shares its connection through ICS, so we choose the first option: "This computer connects directly to the Internet." If, in your case, your computer connects to a router, or shares another computer's Internet connection, instead choose "This computer connects to the Internet through another computer on my network or through a residential gateway." (See Figure 13.6.) Click Next.

Figure 13.6
Select whether your computer connects directly to the Internet, or connects through another computer or a router

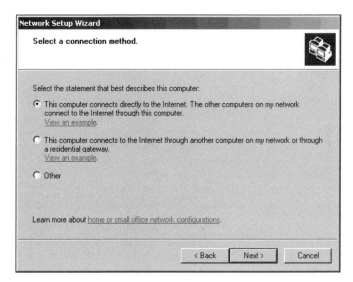

In the next screen (see Figure 13.7), the wizard asks you to choose your default Internet connection (because you might have more than one, including a dial-up Internet account and cable or DSL Internet access). Windows XP takes a guess, but it might not choose the correct connection (it did not, in my case). Choose your connection and click Next.

Figure 13.7
Select your default Internet connection, either the network adapter, or dial-up connection, that you want to use to share Internet access

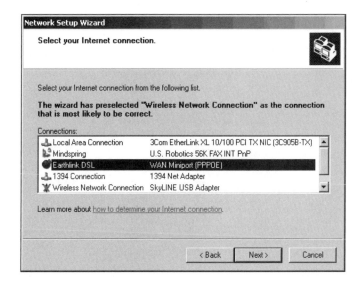

If your computer has more than one network adapter, you can either choose which ones to use for file and Internet sharing, or you can let the Network Setup Wizard handle the job for you. In most cases, the default selection ("Determine the appropriate network connections for me") works just fine. (See Figure 13.8.) Click Next.

Figure 13.8
Choose your network connections or let Windows XP do it for you

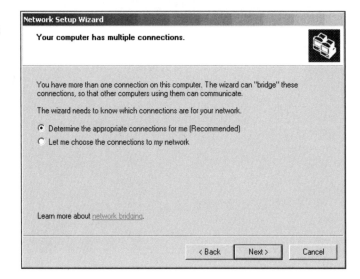

Now, it's time to choose a name and a description for your computer, as shown in Figure 13.9. If you use a cable modem, your ISP might determine the name you use. I name my computers after aircraft carriers, but that's just me. Name them anything you'll remember. The name should be one word without spaces. The description can be several words and can include spaces.

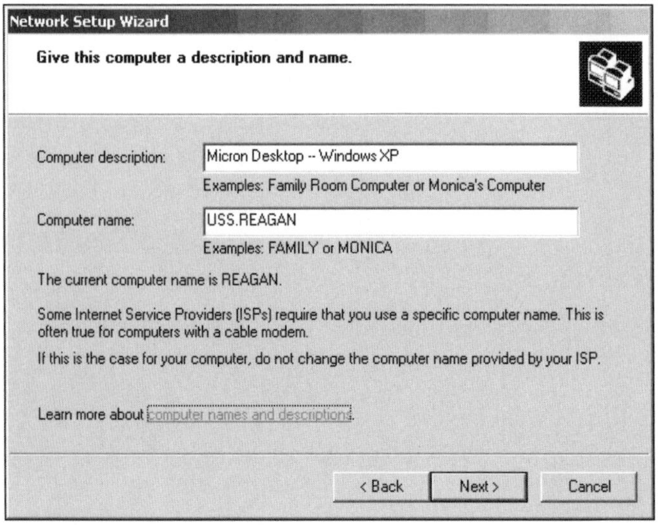

Figure 13.9
Give your computer a name and provide a description

Choose your workgroup name. The default workgroup name is MSHOME (as shown in Figure 13.10), but you can change it to anything you want. Make sure the workgroup name is the same on all your computers.

Figure 13.10
Choose a workgroup name

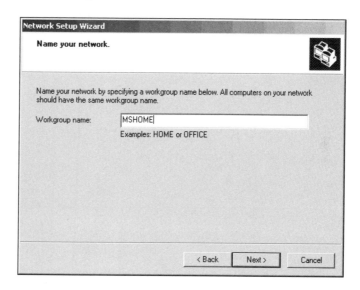

The Network Setup Wizard shows you a list of the options you've selected (see Figure 13.11). Review them to make sure you have everything as you want it. If something is amiss, click the Back button to make your change. Otherwise, click Next.

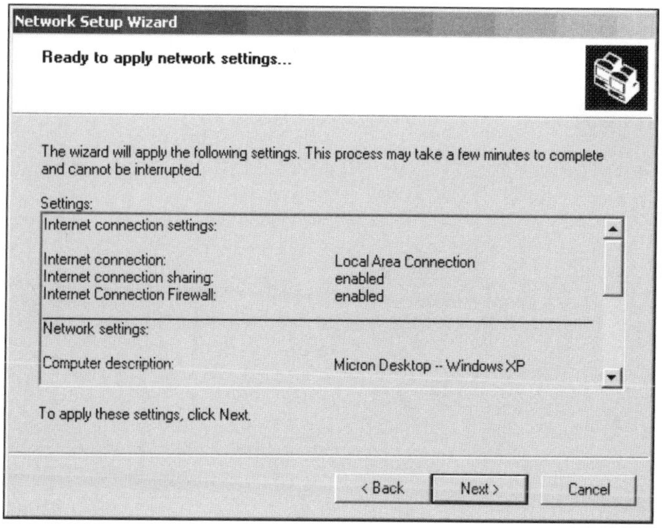

Figure 13.11
Review your network settings

Wait while the wizard configures your network settings. The Network Setup Wizard goes to work (see Figure 13.12).

Figure 13.12
Grab a drink while the
Network Setup Wizard
applies the settings
you've chosen in the
previous steps

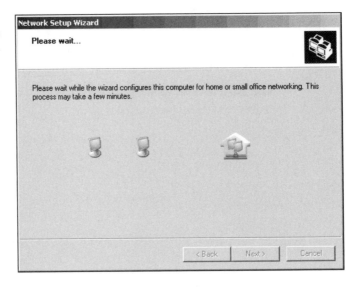

To match the settings for this machine on all your other computers, you can create a
network setup floppy disk. After this disk is created, you can install the software on it at
each of your other PCs. Select Create a Network Setup Disk (as shown in Figure 13.13)
and follow the directions. Or, you can skip this step and go to the next, if you have the
Windows XP Home disk handy.

Figure 13.13
Get started creating a
Network Setup Disk

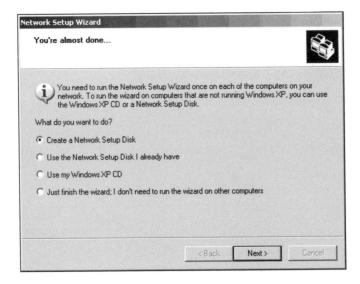

Another option is to use your Windows XP Home CD-ROM to install the Network Setup
Wizard on your other machines. Insert the CD-ROM into the hard drive of any computer

that doesn't have the Network Startup Wizard (Windows 95 and 98 computers). Click the "Perform additional tasks" button (see Figure 13.14).

Figure 13.14
The Windows XP CD-ROM offers the Network Setup Wizard for your Windows 95/98 machines; select "Perform additional tasks"

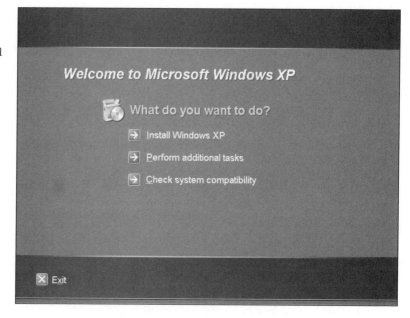

Now, click "Set up a home or small office network." (See Figure 13.15.)

Figure 13.15
Launch the Network Setup Wizard

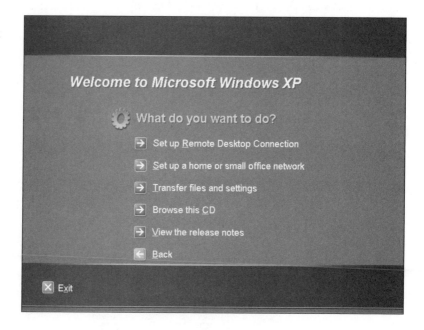

The Network Setup Wizard dialog box opens. Click Yes to start installing files the wizard needs to configure your computer to access the network, as shown in Figure 13.16.

Figure 13.16
Click Yes

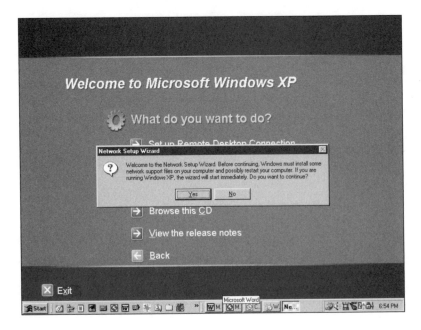

The Network Setup Wizard warns you that you will be prompted to restart your computer. Close any work or applications you might have open. Click OK. (See Figure 13.17.)

Figure 13.17
Prepare to restart

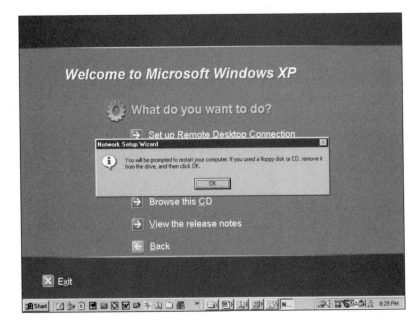

You are prompted to restart your computer. Click Yes, as shown in Figure 13.18. Eject your Windows XP CD-ROM.

Figure 13.18
Restart your computer

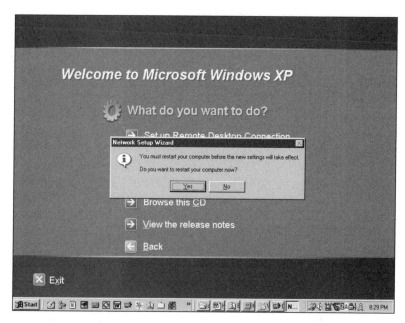

After you restart your computer, the Network Setup Wizard automatically launches. Follow the Network Setup Wizard's prompts, just as you did on your Windows XP machine. (See Figure 13.19.) Click Next to get started.

Figure 13.19
Step through the
Network Setup Wizard

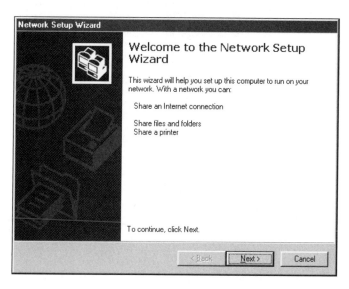

When you reach the "Connect a setup method" screen, choose "This computer connects to another computer in my network or through a residential gateway" (see Figure 13.20). This sets up the Windows 98 computer to connect to the Windows XP computer we configured in the first steps.

Figure 13.20
Select a connection method

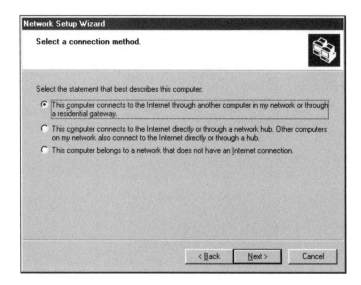

When you're done, click Finish (see Figure 13.21). Your computer should now be ready to share file and Internet access with your Windows XP computer.

Figure 13.21
Click Finish to save your network configuration settings

Appendix A

Growing Your Network, a Visual Guide

This appendix functions as a visual guide to various network setup configurations. The illustrations show you how you can build up your network, adding equipment as you need it, over time. For each setup, you see how the hardware is connected, what components you need, and some of the benefits and drawbacks of each configuration.

With the proper care and attention, your network can grow as your needs grow.

Connect Two Computers

You can directly connect two computers together through an Ethernet crossover cable. You cannot use a regular patch (a.k.a. a straight-through cable) to connect two computers directly. If you think you'll add another computer later, use a hub and regular patch cables instead of a crossover cable.

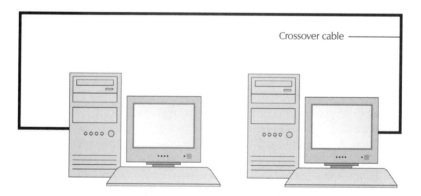

Crossover cable

▶ **Hardware you'll need**. A crossover cable and network adapters for both computers.

► **Benefits**. An inexpensive way to connect computers directly together; simple to set up.

► **Drawbacks**. A crossover cable won't be of any use if you add more than two computers to your network. If you think you'll *ever* need to network three computers, buy an inexpensive hub and check out the next scenario.

Connect Three Computers with a Hub

You can connect three computers, via Ethernet, by way of an inexpensive hub and patch cables. You can purchase a four-port hub starting at about $40.

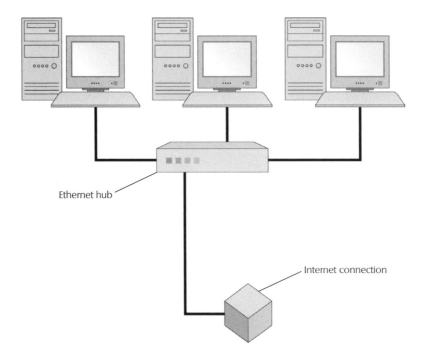

► **Hardware you'll need**. Ethernet network adapters for each computer, a hub, and three Ethernet patch cables.

► **Benefits**. A simple configuration that is easy to set up and allows you to expand your network by plugging more computers into the hub as your network grows. You can also, later, plug a wireless access point into the hub to provide more flexibility, such as a laptop computer that connects to the network from anywhere in your house. We look at adding wireless capability later in this appendix.

▶ **Drawbacks**. Not as flexible as no-new-wires home networking technologies, such as phoneline and powerline.

Connect Three Computers to the Internet

You can also use an Ethernet network to allow three computers to share a modem connection to the Internet through one computer (we call this the primary computer). The primary computer shares its connection to the Internet through Windows Internet Connection Sharing (ICS), a free component of Windows 98 Second Edition and later PCs.

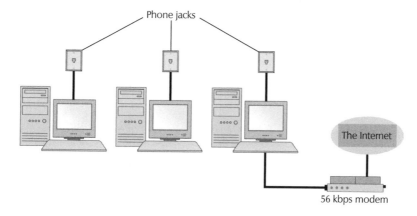

▶ **Hardware you'll need**. Phoneline network adapters for each PC, regular phone cables to connect the network adapters to phone jacks, and a 56 kbps modem connected to one computer.

▶ **Benefits**. Phoneline network adapters are relatively inexpensive (less than $50 per adapter). You don't need a hub—your house phone wiring connects your computers together. The best part is you don't need to string cable to each computer you want to connect, as you do with Ethernet—a free phone jack does the trick.

▶ **Drawbacks**. Phoneline networks are not as fast as Ethernet. You probably don't have a phone jack in each room of your house, in which case a powerline network might work better.

Add a Broadband (Cable or DSL) Modem

For faster Internet access, you can add a cable or DSL modem. Now, each computer has Internet access, and you don't need to tie up the phone line when surfing the Net. Again, the primary computer shares its Internet access using ICS.

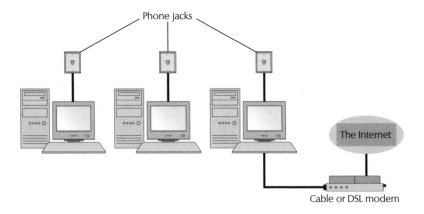

Phone jacks

The Internet

Cable or DSL modem

▶ **Hardware you'll need**. A cable or DSL modem and an Ethernet cable to connect the modem to the network adapter in your primary computer. You need *two* network adapters for the primary machine: one to plug in the cable modem and another for connecting to the network. A USB Ethernet adapter can be helpful in this situation, so that you don't have to install two PCI Ethernet cards (by opening up your computer). You can also use a USB wireless, phoneline, or powerline adapter to get around the two-network card requirement. Or, you can purchase a cable (or DSL) modem with a USB connection.

▶ **Benefits**. Everyone in the house gets to share fast Internet access—no more tying up the phone line.

▶ **Drawbacks**. You need two network adapters to get the job done.

Use a Router to Share Internet Access

You can also create an Ethernet network with a router to share the cable modem between all the computers. Now, each computer has Internet access, but you don't need to leave a computer on, as in the previous scenario, to get online. The router takes the place of ICS.

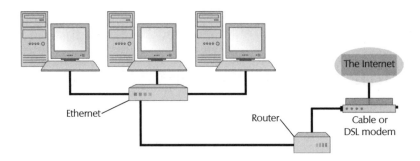

The Internet

Ethernet

Router

Cable or
DSL modem

▶ **Hardware you'll need.** Network adapters for each computer, a cable or DSL modem, a hub, a router, and patch cables for connecting each network adapter and the router to the hub. You can also purchase a router that has a built-in hub.

▶ **Benefits.** A router lets you share Internet access among all your computers, and provides security for your network, especially if your router has a built-in firewall.

▶ **Drawbacks**. Added expense over using Windows ICS (but well worth it).

Use a Wireless Access Point

In this scenario, you can connect computers wirelessly using 802.11b network adapters and a wireless access point with a built-in router. The access point allows you to use a laptop that can roam around the house and maintain a network and Internet connection.

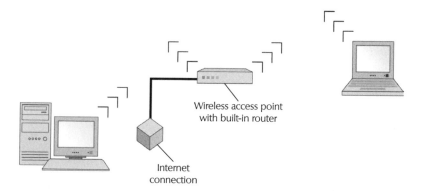

Wireless access point
with built-in router

Internet
connection

▶ **Hardware you'll need.** A wireless access point and a wireless network adapter for each computer you want to connect wirelessly. If you have not yet set up your network, consider a wireless access point with a built-in router, and potentially, a built-in hub. You need powerline network adapters for each computer you want to connect by electical outlets.

▶ **Benefits.** Extends the reach of your network to about 150 feet around the house, the range of most wireless network equipment.

▶ **Drawbacks**. Wireless equipment is more expensive than its wired counterparts. Some rooms in your house might be too far apart from each other to make wireless access a reliable network option. If your rooms are quite far from each other, consider a phone or powerline bridge, as we look at in the next section.

APPENDIX A

Create a Hybrid Network

A phone or powerline bridge allows you to connect phoneline and powerline networking equipment to an Ethernet network. You can then add a computer to your network anywhere in the house with a phone jack or electrical outlet. Adding a wireless access point lets you connect computers wirelessly to the network. In this scenario, we also use a switch, which provides faster data transfer than a hub between the wireless and wired segments of the network.

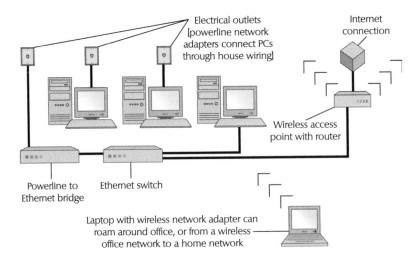

Electrical outlets [powerline network adapters connect PCs through house wiring]

Internet connection

Wireless access point with router

Powerline to Ethernet bridge

Ethernet switch

Laptop with wireless network adapter can roam around office, or from a wireless office network to a home network

▶ **Hardware you'll need**. A phone or powerline bridge and a patch cable to connect the bridge to your hub. Your existing house wiring takes care of the cabling from your hub to your computer. You also need a wireless access point with a built-in router and a broadband Internet connection.

▶ **Benefits**. No need to string new wires through your house to add a computer to the network. You can easily move a computer to a new room (or a new house) and just plug in to a wall jack to connect the computer to your network. Wireless networking hardware offers roaming capability.

▶ **Drawbacks**. Phoneline equipment is inexpensive (though more expensive than Ethernet). Powerline network adapters are very expensive, because the technology is new.

Add a Multimedia Device or Print Server

You can add stand-alone devices (that do not need to be connected to a PC) to your network that increase its usefulness and your enjoyment of it. An MP3 player can add to your network a high-tech jukebox with access to your favorite music from any computer in your house. A print server can manage your printing jobs, sending prints to the appropriate printer when one becomes available.

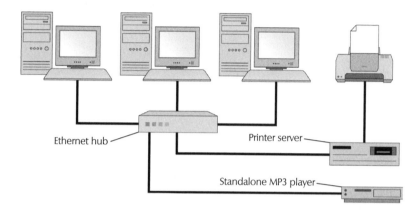

Ethernet hub

Printer server

Standalone MP3 player

▶ **Hardware you'll need**. A standalone media device and patch cable.

▶ **Benefits**. You can add components to your network without connecting them to your PCs, freeing up ports and giving you more choice about where to place your standalone network components.

▶ **Drawbacks**. Cost. Standalone components add to the expense of your network. Printer servers run $100-150 and MP3 players cost in the range of $800-1500.

Appendix B
Glossary

802.11a

The newest wireless networking standard, which has a maximum speed of 54 mbps. 802.11a is a good choice for both video and audio. Manufacturers claim the technology is five times faster than 802.11b, though the networks do not consistently operate at these speeds. Still, 802.11a is currently the best choice for wireless networking that carries multimedia.

802.11b

The most popular wireless networking standard. The technology carries data at a maximum of 11 mbps.

Ad Hoc Mode

A wireless network that allows the network adapter cards to communicate directly with each other. (Wireless networks can work in one of two ways: ad hoc mode or infrastructure mode.) In a small area, you might do well to use ad hoc mode, also called peer-to-peer.

Analog Modem

A device that converts digital signals from your computers to analog signals that can be carried over a phone line. Most computers today come with 56 kbps analog modems.

Autonegotiating

A hub or network adapter that can transmit data at either 10 mbps or 100 mbps.

Bandwidth

The speed at which data travels over your network. Bandwidth is often described in kilobits (kbps) and megabits per second (mbps).

Bit

The smallest amount of data a computer can store, a zero or one. One alphanumeric character (such as a number, letter, or special character) is made up of eight bits, which equals one byte. The speed of most network equipment is measured in megabits per second (mbps).

Byte

A measurement equaling eight bits.

Cable Modem

The most popular means of getting broadband Internet access to a home. Cable modems use the same cable line that you use to plug in a TV.

Client-Server Network

A network that uses a central computer, called a server, for storing files or programs that everyone can share—a popular network in many offices. A server-based network is often called a client-server network.

Crossover Cable

A special cable that allows you to connect one network adapter directly to another, without the use of a hub. A crossover cable is helpful if you don't want to set up a whole network, but instead want to connect only two computers.

Data Transfer Rate

The maximum speed at which data can move across your network; often referred to as bandwidth or throughput.

Dave

A program from Thursby Software that allows Macs to share files and printers on a PC network.

DHCP

(Dynamic Host Configuration Protocol) A way to automatically distribute IP addresses to each computer on your network—offered on many routers. DHCP saves you from having to enter your IP address manually on each computer.

DSL

(Digital Subscriber Line) A method of providing high-speed Internet access, using regular phone lines, to your home.

Encryption

A form of security that encodes data by combining the data you want to keep safe typically through a mathematical algorithm, so that even if someone should gain access to it, they won't be able to read and understand the data.

Ethernet

A standard, sometimes called an architecture, for network communication and, more casually, what most people call networks that use Ethernet hardware. The cabling for an Ethernet network looks a lot like a telephone cable, but is thicker, and has eight wires inside instead of four. The cheapest and most often used Ethernet network hardware is called 10BaseT, which transmits data at up to 10 mbps (megabits per second). Newer, more expensive Ethernet hardware, called 100BaseT, transmits data at 100 mbps.

Fast Ethernet

A standard for network communication, also called 100BastT, that transmits data at a maximum of 100mbps. (*See* Ethernet.)

Firewall

A form of security that blocks unauthorized access to your PC over the Internet. A firewall can also check to make sure data sent from your computer is authorized. Some firewalls offer protection from viruses which send e-mails, for instance, from your address book, without your knowledge.

HomePNA

A home networking standard, also called phoneline networking, that lets you use your existing house telephone wiring to connect your network.

HomeRF

A wireless networking technology that is considered by many to be better suited to multimedia than Wi-Fi (802.11b). HomeRF uses a different technology than Wi-Fi, which gives priority to multimedia transmissions, providing them with more bandwidth so that audio and video come across cleanly.

HomeRF 2.0

The second generation of the HomeRF standard, which is slightly slower than Wi-Fi (10 mbps rather than 11 mbps).

Hot Swap

A term referring to equipment that can be plugged into ports while the computer is on.

Hub

A networking hardware device that allows you to connect as many computers to your network as the hub has available ports (usually four to sixteen).

Infrastructure Mode

A wireless network in which the wireless network adapters communicate with a wireless hub, called an access point. (*See* Ad-Hoc Mode.)

ICS

(Internet Connection Sharing) A software router built-in Windows 98 Second Edition and later Windows operating systems. ICS lets one of the computers on your network share its Internet connection with all the other computers on your LAN.

IP Address

A unique number that identifies each computer on a network, including the Internet. IP addresses are in the format of four sets of numbers, separated by periods, such as 192.168.x.x. A static IP address provided by your Internet Service Provider (ISP) is an IP address that does not change. A dynamic IP address changes at your ISP's discretion, and allows the ISP to allocate IP addresses as users sign on.

ISP

Internet Service Provider.

Kilobit

A measurement equaling one thousand bits. Most cable and DSL modem connection speeds are measured in kilobits per second (kbps).

Latency

The time between the request for information and when it starts to download.

LAN

(Local Area Network) A network within one home or office is often called a LAN.

Megabit

A measurement equaling one million bits. Some fast Internet connections carry data at 1.5 megabits per second (mbps) or faster. An 802.11b network can transmit data at up to 11 mbps. USB hardware has a maximum speed of 12 mbps. Fast Ethernet can transfer data at up to 100 mbps.

NAT

(Network Address Translation) A feature used by routers, which allows you to share one IP address, provided by your ISP, among all the computers on your network.

Network Adapter

A device you plug into a PC that enables communication between computers. Network adapters are sometimes called NICs, or Network Interface Cards.

NIC

Network Interface Card. (*See* Network Adapter.)

Null-Modem Cable

A special type of serial cable that allows you to connect two computers directly together to transfer files.

Parallel Port

A 25-pin socket found on computers for connecting printers, scanners, and other devices. Data in a parallel port is transmitted in parallel, more than one bit at a time. Using a special parallel cable, such as those available by Parallel Technologies (lpt.com) and LapLink Inc. (www.laplink.com), you can make direct cable connections and transfer data between two computers.

Patch Cables

The cables used to connect Ethernet network adapters and hubs.

PC Card

A small device (also called a PCMCIA card) that allows you to connect peripherals, such as a wireless network card, or a miniature hard drive, to laptops. A PC Card slides into the PC Card slot on the side of a laptop. For adding a laptop to your network, installing a PC Card is as simple as installing a USB card, and a PC Card takes up less space.

PCI

(Peripheral Component Interconnect) A slot for installing peripherals. Installing a PCI network adapter is slightly more tricky than installing a USB network adapter. You need to take the case off your computer and find an open PCI slot to install the network card. People who are comfortable installing hardware in their computers might favor a PCI network adapter because, once you install it, there's no chance of accidentally pulling it out and disconnecting your connection. In addition, the USB ports on some computers (there are usually two) are found on the front of the computer.

PCMACLAN

A program from Miramar Systems for sharing data and printers from a Macintosh on a PC network.

Peer-to-Peer Network

A network in which the computers connect to each other directly.

PGP

(Pretty Good Privacy) A two-key encryption system. You make one key public, by uploading it to a server or e-mailing it to someone. People use your public key to encrypt data, such as e-mail messages, they want to send to you. Your private key, which you keep secret, is used to decrypt the scrambled messages into text that you can read.

Powerline

The networking products that send data over the electrical wiring in your house. The powerline networking standard, which transmits data at up to 14 mbps, is called HomePlug (www.homeplug.com).

Print Server

A computer or a stand-alone hardware device that controls the printing jobs on a network. A printer server can share multiple printers, queuing jobs as they are received and sending them to a printer when one is ready.

Protocol

A set of rules that establishes how computers communicate.

RJ-45

The connectors used in Ethernet networks. They look like, but are slightly larger than, regular telephone connectors.

Router

A device that lets one network communicate with another. In most cases in home networking, this means connecting the computer network at your house (your LAN) to the very large network called the Internet.

Serial Port

A hardware interface that sends data one bit at a time. Serial ports are sometimes called RS-232 ports or COM (communication) ports.

SSID

(Service Set Identifier) A string of text that identifies your wireless network and must be entered into the configuration software for each adapter or access point. You need to enter the same SSID on your network adapters and access point, or your network adapters won't be able to communicate with each other.

TCP/IP

(Transmission Control Protocol over Internet Protocol) The protocol, or language, of the Internet. You can use TCP/IP as your home network's protocol, which allows you to set up file, printer, and Internet sharing over your LAN.

Throughput

The maximum speed at which data can move across your network. Often referred to as bandwidth or data transfer rate.

USB

(Universal Serial Bus) A connector that allows you to plug into ports you probably already have in your computer, if you bought your PC later than 1995.

UTP

(Unshielded Twisted Pair) An inexpensive cable, which is used for both networks and phone wiring.

WAN

(Wide Area Network) A large network that connects many, often geographically distant, networks. The Internet is a WAN.

WEP

(Wired Equivalent Privacy) A security protocol that encodes and decodes the information transferred over your wireless network. If you are concerned about someone accessing your data, enable WEP.

Wi-Fi

A standard set by a wireless industry association called the Wireless Ethernet Compatibility Alliance to ensure that 802.11b networking devices work together, even if they are from different manufacturers.

Wireless Access Point

A hardware device that works a bit like a wireless hub and allows multiple computers with wireless network adapters to communicate with each other. An access point also lets you connect a wireless network to a wired one, or to a cable or DSL (Digital Subscriber Line) modem.

WLAN

Wireless Local Area Network.

Appendix C
Network Yellow Pages

Network Resources

When your kitchen sink sprouts a leak, you might open the yellow pages to find a plumber. Likewise, when you need networking help, or buying advice, you can turn to the Web sites listed in the following sections for assistance.

You can use these Web sites to:

▶ Shop for and save money on hardware

▶ Find up-to-date information on new technologies

▶ Help you troubleshoot network problems

▶ Find freeware and shareware downloads (software you can install at no/low cost)

▶ Follow tutorials that can help you install the latest equipment

Public Wireless Local Area Networks (WLANs)

If you use a wireless network adapter and own a laptop, public wireless local area networks can be a great help when you travel. These services open up their networks, at a per-hour charge, allowing travelers high-speed online access while they're on the road.

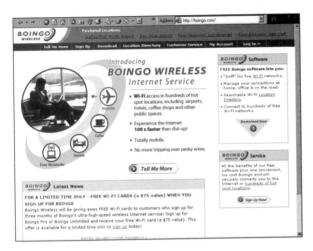

Boingo (www.boingo.com)

Boingo lets you search by location to find where the company offers installed public wireless 802.11b access.

Joltage Broadband Wireless (www.joltage.com)

Joltage offers wireless broadband Internet access at restaurants, hotels, and health clubs.

MobileStar (www.mobilestar.com)

MobileStar is another company providing wireless Internet access, at about $30 a month, at airports, coffee shops, and hotel lounges.

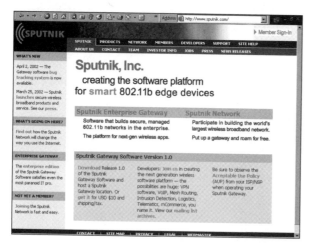

Sputnik (www.sputnik.com)

Sputnik is a free service that helps you find free public access (mostly in metropolitan areas) to wireless 802.11b networks.

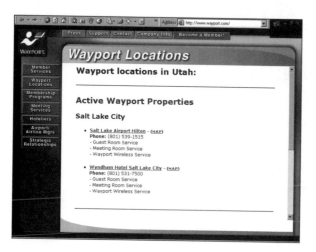

Wayport (www.wayport.com)

Wayport provides wireless LAN access at airports and hotels. The company also offers fast, wired Ethernet network connections at their business centers in 13 airports.

Gaming Sites

Gaming sites can help you find games to play online, such as arcade and downloadable 3D games, as well as find partners for all sorts of diversions, including online board and card games.

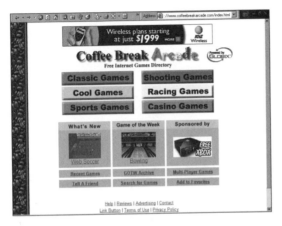

Coffee Break Arcade (www.coffeebreakarcade.com)

Coffee Break Arcade lists games that are hosted on various Web sites. The site provides game descriptions, instructions on how to play, and direct links that start the games.

Gamepen (gamepen.ugo.com)

Gamepen offers reviews, game tips, and downloads.

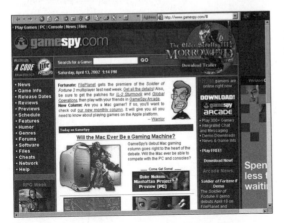

GameSpy (www.gamespy.com)

Like Gamepen, this site offers advice and reviews of all sorts of games.

Entertainment Software Ratings Board (www.esrb.org)

The Software Ratings Board offers searchable game listings. You can find game ratings online, which might help as you decide which games are right for your kids.

EA.com (Electronic Arts)

EA.com offers driving games, sports games, and other 3D games you can play with others or by yourself.

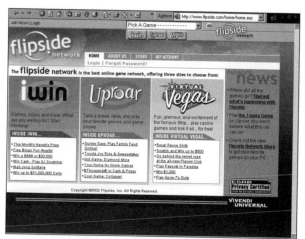

Flipside (www.flipside.com)

The Flipside site, brought to you by the same folks that produce Uproar, offers Vegas-style games (with no wagering), cash prizes for lottery games, and a treasure hunt.

MSN Gaming Zone (www.zone.com)

The Zone, like Yahoo, provides broad offerings. Unlike Yahoo, MSN hosts action and adventure games as well as Sims (simulators), such as Fighter Ace, a pay for play game.

Uproar (www.uproar.com)

Uproar hosts a large collection of familiar TV game shows, including Family Feud and Name That Tune.

Yahoo (games.yahoo.com)

Like other Yahoo offerings, Yahoo's game sites trade fancy graphics for speed and reliability. If you enjoy board and card games, Yahoo is the place to be.

Shockwave.com (www.shockwave.com)

Shockwave.com offers some of the best gaming around—at file sizes that won't make you suffer through interminable downloads. Shockwave is a program, from software-maker Macromedia, that you install on your computer so that you can view multimedia.

BBC (www.bbc.co.uk/games)

The BBC is another gaming site with a cool English bent, including online versions of British game shows.

id Software (www.idsoftware.com)

id Software is the maker of the popular multiplayer game Quake (and its sequels, including Quake III Arena). You can find available Quake servers on the Internet and more information about multiplayer Quake at www.stomped.com.

Music

Whether you're looking for music to play over your network or audio software to play your tunes, these sites can help.

MP3.com (www.mp3.com)

MP3.com offers all sorts of downloads for music fans, including songs and audio software. Songs are classified by format.

Nullsoft Winamp (www.winamp.com)

One of the most widely used MP3 players around is Winamp. You can choose the look of your player by installing free, downloadable interface themes called "skins."

Windows Media Player (www.microsoft.com/windows/windowsmedia)

You can find the most recent version of the free Windows Media Player here. The player is useful for listening to MP3, WMA (Windows Media), and other music files.

RealPlayer (www.real.com)

RealNetworks' RealPlayer is handy for listening to music files you copy to your hard drive, as well as streaming media, such as archived radio programs. Like the Windows Media Player, RealPlayer handles both audio and video files.

Instant Messaging

Instant messaging is a fun way to stay in touch with friends and another way to get use out of your network. All of the programs listed here are free to use.

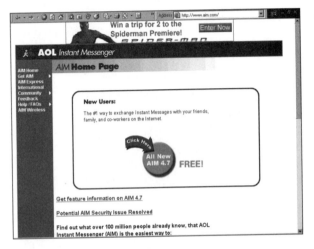

AOL Instant Messenger (www.aim.com)

America Online offers its very popular AOL Instant Messenger, which lets you chat with AOL users as well as anyone else who signs up for a free account.

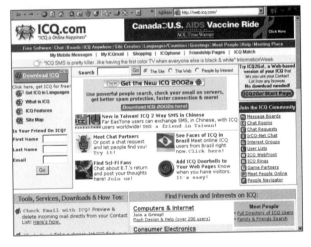

ICQ (www.icq.com)

Owned by AOL, ICQ is another very popular IM client. ICQ offers more features and a slightly more complicated interface than AOL Instant Messenger.

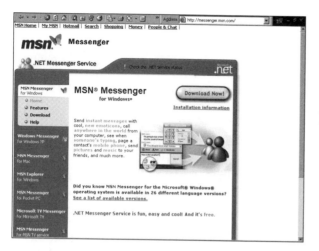

MSN Messenger (messenger.msn.com)

You can use MSN Messenger to send instant messages to other MSN Messenger users. The program is free to download and available for PCs and Macs.

Yahoo Messenger (messenger.yahoo.com)

Got a Yahoo account? If so, consider Yahoo Messenger, another free download that combines features of Yahoo's other services, such as e-mail alerts and news/portfolio tracking, into this instant messenger.

Video

You can download movie players, such as WinDVD (download at www.intervideo.com), to watch a movie on your computer's DVD drive (if you have one). However, the program doesn't allow you to open a DVD that's not on a local drive. It's just not set up to handle the task. The movie industry also puts copy protections on DVDs, which makes the process of playing a DVD from one machine to another on the network even more difficult.

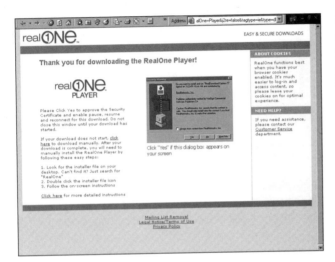

RealNetworks' RealPlayer (www.real.com)

RealNetworks' audio and video player is one of the most widely used Internet-based video players around. You can use the most recent version, called the RealOne player, to watch movie trailers, video shorts, and all sorts of other video content. You can find directories of Internet video at the RealNetworks site. The RealOne player is offered in a free version and pay version that offers more features.

QuickTime (www.apple.com/quicktime)

QuickTime is Apple's video file format. Many of the feature film trailers you find on the Web require QuickTime software.

Windows Media Player (www.microsoft.com/ windows/windowsmedia)

The Windows Media Player comes bundled with all recent versions of Microsoft Windows. The Player is updated frequently. You can download the most recent version at the Microsoft site.

Multimedia Networking

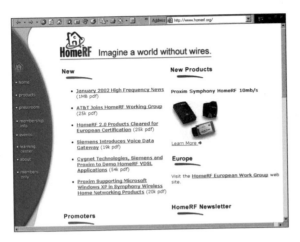

HomeRF (www.homerf.org)

HomeRF is a wireless networking standard that competes with 802.11b (also called Wi-Fi). The technology is capable of working with cordless phones and is cited for its deft handling of multimedia, despite a slower maximum speed (10 mbps) than 802.11b (11 mbps).

SnapStream (www.snapstream.com)

This software lets you copy TV programs to your hard drive then share them over a network.

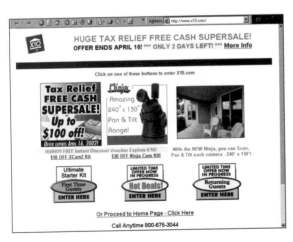

X-10 (www.x10.com)

X-10 is known for products that auto-mate appliances over home electrical wiring and for its ubiquitous pop-up ads. The company makes wireless video and audio products.

Direct Cable Connections and Remote Access

You can connect two PCs together using Windows software and a special cable. The companies listed in the following sections provide both software and the cables you need to make this connection.

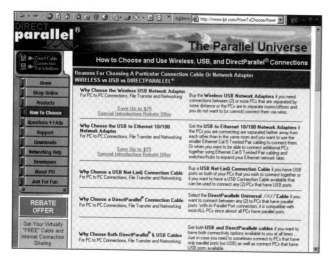

Parallel Technologies (www.lpt.com)

Parallel Technologies sells parallel and USB cables you can purchase for connecting two computers together.

Symantec's pcAnywhere (www.symantec.com)

pcAnywhere provides remote access software for connections by cable, modem, network, and over the Internet.

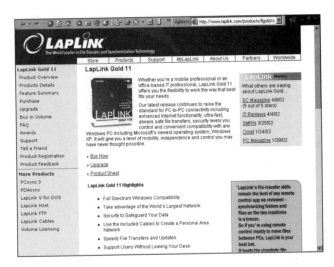

Traveling Software's LapLink (www.laplink.com)

Traveling Software's LapLink also offers remote access features and the capability to transfer files from one computer to another using a special cable.

Security

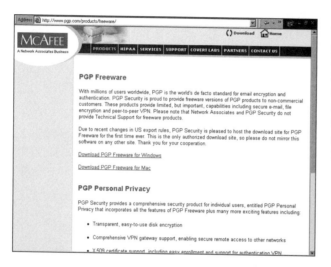

PGP *(www.pgp.com/ products/freeware)*

PGP (Pretty Good Privacy) is a method of encoding your data, such as your e-mails, so that someone can encrypt a message that only you can read. You can also find the latest version of PGP at www.pgpi.org.

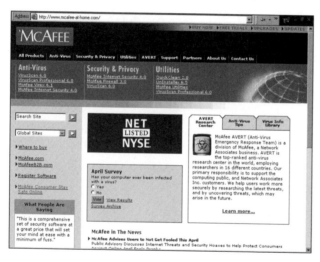

McAfee *(www.mcafee-at-home.com)*

McAfee, owned by Network Associates, offers firewall, antivirus, and bundled software packages that offer protection for your computers.

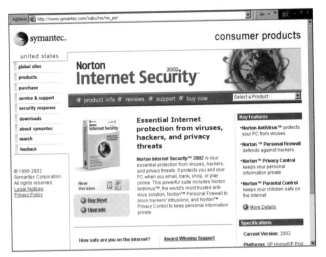

Symantec (www.symantec.com)

Symantec offers firewall and antivirus products, including Norton AntiVirus and Norton Internet Security, which includes a personal firewall, as well as ad blocking and Web content filtering.

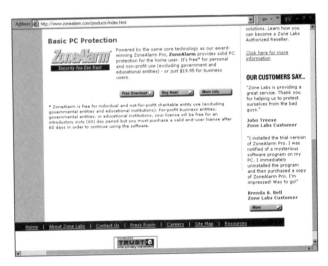

ZoneAlarm (www.zonealarm.com)

ZoneAlarm is a personal firewall from Zone Labs (www.zonealarm.com) that's free for personal use. A commercial version of ZoneAlarm is also available, which offers more features, such as ad and cookie blocking, for $50.

Network Hardware Vendors

Some common network adapter vendors and their download sites (where you can find up-to-date drivers) are included in the following list. We've tried to point you to the main support and download pages, but if you have trouble reaching any of the sites, try their homepages (www.intel.com, for instance, rather than support.intel.com).

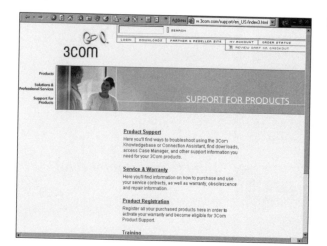

3Com (support.3com.com)

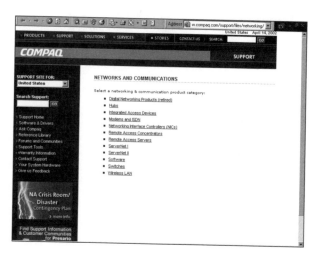

Compaq (www.compaq.com/ support/files/networking)

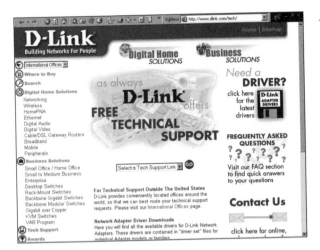

D-Link (www.dlink.com/tech)

Intel (support.intel.com)

Linksys (www.linksys.com/download)

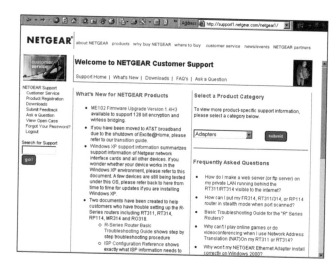

Netgear
(support1.netgear.com/
netgear1)

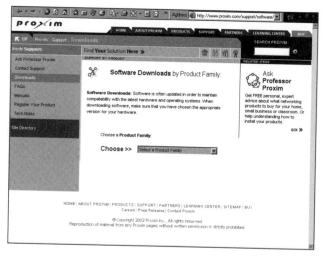

Proxim (www.proxim.com/
support/software)

Network Tips and Troubleshooting

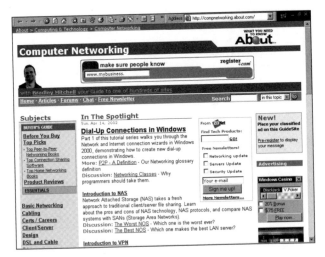

About.com (compnetworking.about.com)

About.com is known for helping users find information on all sorts of topics. The networking section of the site provides a good jumping off point to additional information. Here, you'll find networking articles, advice, and an extensive collection of links to other helpful networking sites.

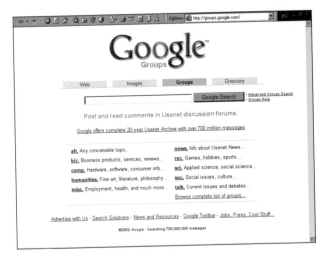

Google Groups (groups.google.com)

Not network specific, but very helpful, the newsgroup search at Google Groups can be a lifesaver. You can search across many Internet discussion groups for answers to your network installation questions. The group's comp.networks and comp.os. ms-windows. networking.misc are both good places to wander through as you start planning your network.

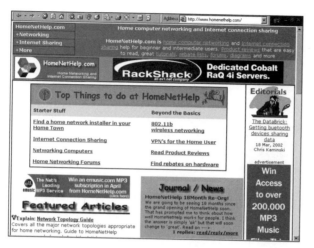

HomeNetHelp.com (www.homenethelp.com)

HomeNetHelp.com offers excellent step-by-step tutorials, reviews, and user forums where you can trade stories of setup headaches—and find help—from other network troubleshooters like yourself.

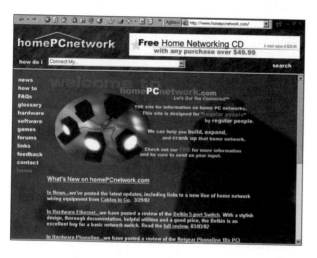

homePCnetwork.com (www.homepcnetwork.com)

HomePCnetwork.com is another good site that can help you with Macs and PCs.

MacWindows (www.macwindows.com)

For more complex jobs, check out the MacWindows Web site—the site offers tips for getting all flavors of Macs and Windows talking to each other.

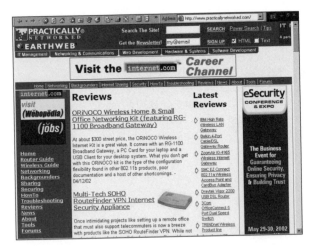

Practically Networked (www.practicallynet-worked. com)

This is another great site for finding help in a pinch. The site has how-to and troubleshooting sections that can help you with installation of wired and wireless networks. Practically Networked also has user forums (you must register first to use them) where you can scratch your head (virtually) with other folks who might have found the solution to your problem.

PCWorld.com (www.pcworld.com)

PC World offers great advice and tutorials for all manner of PC issues, including purchasing and installing network equipment for homes and small offices.

TechWeb.com (www.techWeb.com)

TechWeb.com is a consistently useful site for learning about networking and finding the latest products available.

Web Servers

Windows 98 includes the Personal Web Server. You can download the program for other Windows operating systems. Apple Macintosh OS X runs a built-in version of the Apache Web Server. You can download a Microsoft version of the Apache server from the address that follows.

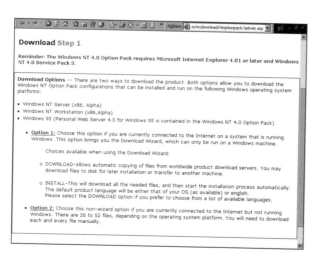

Microsoft Personal Web Server (www.microsoft.com/ msdownload/ ntoptionpack/askwiz.asp)

The PWS is available on the Windows 98 CD, but you can also download it.

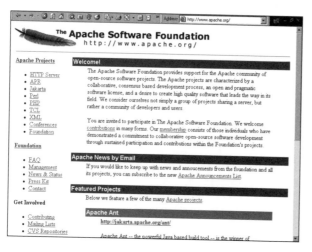

Apache (www.apache.org)

Apache offers a free Web server that works on Windows, UNIX, OS/2, Novell NetWare, and BeOS.

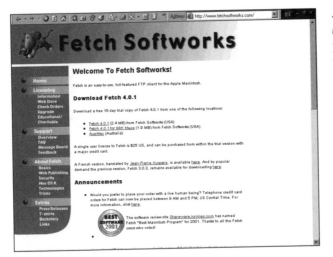

Fetch
(www.fetchsoftworks.com)

Fetch is a popular File Transfer Protocol (FTP) program for Macs, which allows you to copy files to, and download files from, a Web or FTP server.

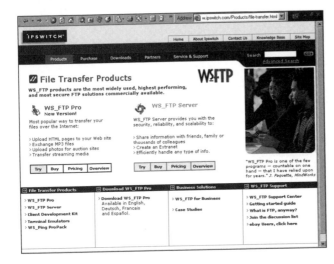

WS_FTP
(www.ipswitch.com)

WS_FTP is a popular FTP program for PCs, used to upload files to a Web or FTP server.

Index

INDEX

T

U

INDEX

X